Lecture Notes of the Institute for Computer Sciences, Social Informatics and Telecommunications Engineering 113

Jaime Lloret Mauri
Joel J.P.C. Rodrigues (Eds.)

Green Communication and Networking

Second International Conference
GreeNets 2012
Gandia, Spain, October 25-26, 2012
Revised Selected Papers

 Springer

Volume Editors

Jaime Lloret Mauri
Universidad Politecnica de Valencia
46022 Valencia, Spain
E-mail: jlloret@dcom.upv.es

Joel J.P.C. Rodrigues
University of Beira Interior
6201-001 Covilhã, Portugal
E-mail: joeljr@ieee.org

ISSN 1867-8211   e-ISSN 1867-822X
ISBN 978-3-642-37976-5   e-ISBN 978-3-642-37977-2
DOI 10.1007/978-3-642-37977-2
Springer Heidelberg Dordrecht London New York

Library of Congress Control Number: 2013935877

CR Subject Classification (1998): C.2.0-5, C.2.m, K.4.m, C.4, J.2

Typesetting: Camera-ready by author, data conversion by Scientific Publishing Services, Chennai, India

Printed on acid-free paper

Springer is part of Springer Science+Business Media (www.springer.com)

Preface

Welcome to the Second International Conference on Green Communications and Networking (GreeNets 2012), which was held in Gandia, Spain, during October 25-26, 2012.

This conference tries to explore and explain the scope and challenges of designing, building, and deploying green communications and networking (GreeNets). It aims at being the premier forum for presentation of results on cutting-edge research on GreeNets by bringing together research professionals from diverse fields including green mobile networks, system architectures, networking and communication protocols, applications, test-bed and prototype, traffic balance and energy-efficient cooperation transmission, system and application issues related to GreeNets. The mission of the conference is to share novel basic research ideas as well as experimental applications in the GreeNets area in addition to identifying new directions for future research and development. GreenNets 2012 provided researchers with an excellent opportunity to share their perspectives with others interested in the various aspects of GreeNets. The conference consisted of multiple sessions that covered a broad range of research aspects. We hope that the conference proceedings will serve as a valuable reference to researchers and developers in the area.

The topics that were covered during the conference are the following:

- Communications and Networking:

  - Communication techniques and protocols for green communications and networking
  - Energy-efficient transmission technologies based on cooperation communication
  - Scalable and flexible energy-efficiency mobile network architectures, deployments, and applications

- Energy-Efficient Network Architecture and protocols:

  - Scalability and mobility issues in energy-efficiency cross-layer design
  - MAC Protocols and QoS Designing for mobile networks

- Systems and Technology:

  - Transactions and workflows in green mobile networks
  - Adaptability and stability of green mobile networks
  - Mobile-and multimedia-supported green mobile networks
  - Experimental and test bed studies for energy-efficiency mobile networks, simulation tools

- Energy-efficient Management:

- Energy-efficient traffic balance, cooperation, and management
- Distributed energy-efficiency resource management techniques
- Protocols for cooperative management and control
- Change management, interoperability, and standards

This year, we received submissions from all over the world. All papers received rigorous peer reviews from our Technical Program Committee (TPC). After carefully examining all the received review reports, the TPC only selected very good papers for presentation at the conference and publication in this Springer LNICST volume. We would also like to announce that 23.68% of the submitted papers are published in the proceedings book.

Putting together GreenNets 2012 was a team effort. First of all, we would like to thank the authors for providing the content of the program. We would also like to express our gratitude to the TPC and reviewers, who worked very hard in reviewing papers and providing suggestions for their improvements. Many people have helped make GreeNets 2012 a success. Their dedication and hard work made it possible to organize such a high-quality venue. We would like to thank the Local Arrangements Chairs (Miguel Garcia and Diana Bri) for an outstanding job this year, the excellent venue choice and impeccable organiza-tion, especially in the face of all the financial challenges it had to overcome. In particular we thank TPC Co-chairs Eduardo Nakamura and Liang Zhou. Our sincere thanks go to Special Session Chairs Jose Soler and Vivek S. Deshpande. We would also like to acknowledge our Industry Track Chair, Jose Maria Alcaraz Calero, our Sponsorship and Exibits Chair, Ezendu Ariwa, our Workshop Chair, Javier Aguiar, our Panel Chair, A.v. Senthil Kumar, our Posters Chair, Kay-han Zrar Ghafoor, and our Publication Chair, Foad Dabiri, for their invaluable contributions. Our Web presence was made possible thanks to our Web Chair, Alejandro Canovas, and our visibility worldwide has been possible thanks to our Publicity Chairs, Sandra Sendra and Min Chen.

We would also like to thank our financial sponsor The Institute for Computer Sciences, Social Informatics and Telecommunications Engineering (ICST), tech-nical sponsor CREATE-NET, and the technical cooperation of the European Alliance for Innovation (EAI), for their support in making GreenNets 2012 a successful event. We are also grateful to Ruzanna Najaryan, Dina Shakirova, and Elisa Mendini for their valuable advice and guidance.

Jaime Lloret Mauri
Joel J. P. C. Rodrigues

Organization

Steering Committee Chairs

Athanasios Vasilakos   National Technical University of Athens
(NTUA), Greece

Imrich Chlamtac   Create-Net, Italy

Organizing Committee

General Chairs

Jaime Lloret   Universidad Politécncia de Valencia, Spain

Joel Rodrigues   Institute of Telecommunications, University of
Beira Interior, Portugal

TPC Chairs

Liang Zhou   Nanjing University of Posts and
Telcommunications, China

Eduardo Nakamura   Federal University of Amazonas, Brazil

Industry Track Chair

Jose Maria Alcaraz Calero   HP Laboratories, Bristol, UK

Sponsorship and Exibits Chair

Ezendu Ariwa   London Metropolitan University, UK

Workshop Chair

Javier Aguiar   University of Valladolid, Spain

Special Session Chairs

Jose Soler   Danmarks Tekniske Universitet, Denmark

Vivek S. Deshpande   MIT College of Engineering, Pune, India

Panel Chair

A.v. Senthil Kumar   Hindusthan College of Arts and Science, India

Posters Chair

Kayhan Zrar Ghafoor   Universiti Teknologi Malaysia, Malaysia

Local Chairs

Diana Bri   Universidad Politécncia de Valencia, Spain
Miguel Garcia   Universidad Politécncia de Valencia, Spain

Publicity Chairs

Min Chen   SNU, Korea
Sandra Sendra   Universidad Politécncia de Valencia, Spain

Publication Chair

Foad Dabiri   UCLA Computer Science, CA, USA

Web Chair

Alejandro Canovas   Universidad Politécncia de Valencia, Spain

Technical Program Committee

Foad Dabiri   Google Inc.
Liang Zhou   ParisTech
Milos Stojmenovic   Singidunum University, Serbia
Eduardo Nakamura   Federal University of Amazonas, Brazil
Manuel Gil Pérez   University of Murcia, Spain
Luís Hernández Callejo   Ciemat - Ceder, Spain
Pascal Lorenz   University of Haute-Alsace, France
Sherali Zeadally   University of the District of Columbia, USA
Qing Yang   Montana State University, USA
Anthony Lewis Brooks   Aalborg University, Denmark
Farid Farahmand   Sonoma State University, USA
Jorge Sa Silva   University of Coimbra, Portugal
Artur Ziviani   National Laboratory for Scientific Computing,
                               Brazil
Kai Lin   Dalian University of Technology, China
Tigang Jiang   University of Electronic Science and
                               Technology of China, China
Sabu M. Thampi   Technopark Campus, India
Hung-Yu Wei   National Taiwan University, Taiwan
Emilio Granell Romero   Universidad Politécnica de Valencia, Spain
Baozhi Chen   Rutgers University - New Brunswick, USA
Xiaohu Ge   Huazhong University of Science and
                               Technology, China

Juan M. Lopez-Soler	University of Granada, Spain
David Lizcano	Universidad Politécnica de Madrid and Universidad a Distancia de Madrid, Spain
Kun Hua	Lawrence Technological University, USA
Marc Gilg	University of Haute-Alsace, France
Otman Chakkor	Abdelmalek Essaadi University, Morocco
Mostafa Ezziyyani	Abdelmalek Essaadi University, Morocco
M'hamed Ait Kbir	Abdelmalek Essaadi University, Morocco

Table of Contents

Green Communications and Networking

Carrier-Grade Networks toward the Future
-NGN and Its Issues-

Koichi Asatani

Kogakuin University,
1-24-2 Nishishinjuku, Shinjuku, Tokyo 163-8677 Japan
asatanik@cc.kogakuin.ac.jp

Abstract. Next Generation Network is designed as the next generation carrier-grade network. Reflecting the ICT trends, NGN adopts packet-based network to flexibly accommodate telephony and data traffics. The IP is adopted as the network layer protocol with additional resource and admission control functionalities enabling QoS management. This paper describes global ICT trends, outline of NGN and its issues toward the future.

Keywords: NGN, IMS, QoS, IP telephony, dependability, Future Networks.

1   Introduction

Carrier-grade networks for the future are being developed as Next Generation Networks (NGN). The NGN is a converged solution after the legacy telecom networks by enabling QoS management and controls in IP network as in legacy telecom networks. The NGN supports voice, Internet services and future services which are being and will be developed with flexible and cost effective manners and with high dependability and high security. It also supports third-party applications through the open interface. NGN also provides more flexible access arrangements such as fixed-mobile convergence (FMC) with generalized mobility, and horizontal and vertical roaming as well as improved security.

The concepts and architecture of NGN are described. The current status of NGN implementation in a commercial offer in Japan is touched upon. Issues for the global evolution of NGN are also described, such as IPv6 related issues, impacts of smartphones, global standards and regulations. ITU-T initiated studies on Future Networks. This paper also briefly addresses the relationship between NGN and Future Networks.

2   Trends in ICT

2.1   Voice to Data and Fixed to Mobile

Fixed telephone subscriptions were growing until 2006. After 2007, the subscriptions have been and are being decreasing. Voice traffic was overtaken by data bits in 2000 in general. The mobile data bits outnumbered mobile voice traffic in 2009. [1, 2]

J. Lloret Mauri and J.J.P.C. Rodrigues (Eds.): GreeNets 2012, LNICST 113, pp. 1–15, 2013.
© Institute for Computer Sciences, Social Informatics and Telecommunications Engineering 2013

Circuit switched network are well-designed for voice traffic. According to the data traffic growth, packet switched networks were being introduced in parallel to circuit switched networks. The role of packet switched networks has been increased. Thanks to the innovative development of voice over packet technology enables voice applications supported by packet switched networks. In 1980s, all IP telephone networks were planned and developed to integrate data and voice traffics.

Global ICT development over decade shows drastic changes, thanks to the rapid growth of IP-based data communications such as, cloud computing and big data. All indices of ICT growth are very positive except fixed telephone subscriptions as shown in Figure 1.

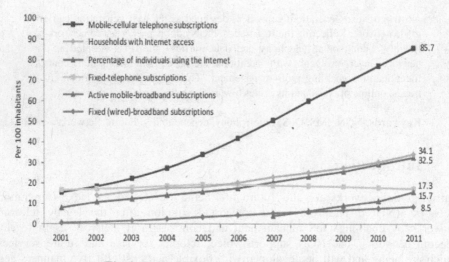

Fig. 1. Global ICT Development 2001-20011 [1]

Mobile telephone subscriptions are over six billion globally by the end of 2011 out of seven billion global population [3]. Internet users are estimated to be over 2.4 billion globally. Both are still growing rapidly [4]. Moreover, the global traffic growth rate is drastically larger than the growth rate in number of mobile devices and Internet users. Typical smartphone traffic is estimated as 35 times larger than typical feature phone traffic.[5]

2.2   Broadband Access and IP Telephony

Real time applications over Internet were enabled thanks to the penetration of broadband access, such as Cables, ADSL and FTTH. ADSL played a major role in broadband access. In Japan, FTTH overtook ADSL in 2006 and plays a leading role in broadband access, as shown in Figure 2.

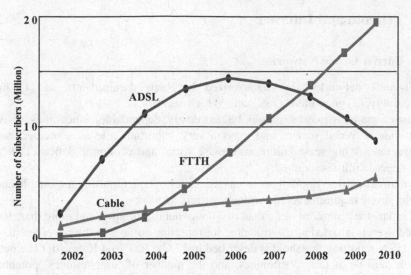

Fig. 2. Broadband Accesses in Japan

IP telephony is one of the most popular real time applications. IP telephone subscriptions are growing with the broadband access penetration.

Two types of IP telephony services are available in Japan. IP telephony with the prefix "*0AB-J*" is a replacement of POTS. IP telephony with the dedicated prefix "*050*" IP telephony supports most POTS services, but it is not connected to some special numbers such as emergency. Total number of IP subscriptions is comparable to POTS subscriptions at the end of 2011, as shown in Figure 3.

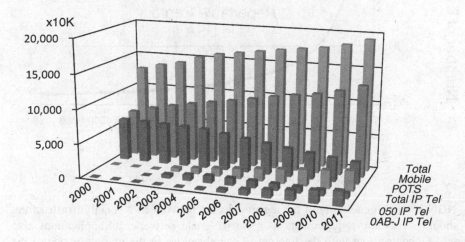

Fig. 3. Telephone Subscriptions in Japan

3   Telecom and Internet

3.1   Carrier Grade Networks

Carrier-grade networks are characterized by such requirements as (1) high-dependability, (2) guaranteed QoS, and (3) high-security.

Carrier grade networks should be extremely dependable, since they provide nation-wide universal service and plays a very important role as a socioeconomic infrastructure. A big scale failure may cause social and economic deficit. The 'five nines' dependability is required.

In many countries, regulations or guidelines for outage reporting are established to keep the severe requirements to common carriers networks.

In Japan, the criteria of more than two hours outage duration and more than 30000 affected users is adopted as the guideline for reporting outages to the government.

In USA, reporting threshold is described in 47 C.F.R. Part 4 Rules [6]. The outage duration must be at least 30 minutes, and the number of 'user-minutes' potentially affected must equal or exceed 900,000, as shown in Figure 4.   The Internet is not ruled by this kind of reporting system. However, the guidelines for VoIP and other IP applications are under discussions.

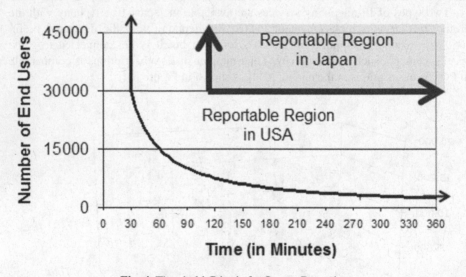

Fig. 4. Threshold Criteria for Outage Reporting

NGN is a new generation of the legacy telecom network as a social infrastructure. It should satisfy the requirements as a carrier grade network. Its applications also should be competitive with the Internet like applications in the market as one of the players.

3.2   Telecom vs. Internet [7]

Principle of the legacy telecom networks is called "network principle". The network operator is responsible for all aspects of the service including user terminals. In most countries, telephone terminals used to be a part of the network operators properties. Users were charged for services provided by the network through the terminals.

Furthermore, the network provides electric power for telephone terminals, so that subscribers could enjoy their service even when the commercial electric power fails, a useful feature in an emergency. In the Internet, the role of IP network is designed as the simple end-to-end packet transport. The end-hosts are responsible for end-to-end information delivery. Thus IP network is named the "stupid network" or "best effort network." The principle is called the "end-to-end principle" [8].

We can also call the telecommunication principle as the "network principle," whereas the Internet principle is the "end principle," given that the end-hosts perform all the functions except that of packet transport.

Operation under the network principle allows the design and management of reliability and dependability, since the terminals as well as network elements are under the responsibility of a single entity, the network operator. Service enhancements and evolutions are generally performed network-wide. As a consequence, the market is mostly monopolistic and stable; service enhancement and evolution are performed in a conservative manner. With the end principle, in contrast, application enhancements and evolutions can be easily achieved without affecting the network infrastructure. Network transparency is therefore required as much as possible, that is, no modification and differentiation of the packets by the network. In practice, complete network transparency is not desirable, because it prevents the differential treatment of packets, including the identification of harmful viruses or attacks, which is detrimental to security.

In telecom networks and the Internet were evolving independently until early 1990s, when World Wide Web (WWW) applications triggered the rapid growth of Internet penetration. Thanks to the development in broadband access technology, such as cable, ADSL and FTTH (Fiber to the Home), Internet could provide real-time and streaming type of applications such as IP telephony and IPTV.

Telecommunication networks are connection-oriented. They support QoS guaranteed, reliable, and dependable services. The charging principle in telecom services is basically usage-based. The Internet is connectionless and provides best-effort type of applications. The charging principle in Internet services is, in general, fixed charging or flat rate.

NGN is designed to be capable of QoS management and controls like in traditional telecommunication networks and to support economical, versatile multimedia applications like those on the current Internet. NGN also provides fixed-mobile convergence (FMC) with generalized mobility, horizontal and vertical roaming as well as improved security.

The "horizontal" handover roaming is the capability of moving among mobile networks of the same technology, for example, from a GSM network to another GSM network, across the boundary of two operators' networks or countries. On the other hand, the handover between two networks using different technologies is called "vertical" roaming, for example, or from/to any cellular network to/from any Wireless Local Area Network (LAN). FMC enables free roaming between fixed and mobile network access.

NGN security is based on the security provided by registration and authentication of user terminals when they request calls. Only registered and authenticated users are allowed access to protect against fake and anonymous communications like spam e-mails that are congesting the current Internet. In specific applications and services, security functions are required in application servers and user terminals.

The advantages of NGN from viewpoints of network operators are as follows:

(1) Cost-effective networks by adopting IP technology as a core transport technology. Having a single core technology enables flexible and efficient network installment and operation, which leads to cost-effective network and service operation.

(2) PSTN emulation/simulation service because telephone service remains a basic pillar application, even while it is expected that the importance of data traffic will grow in time.

(3) More competitive presence in market places globally by enabling FMC and by providing the so-called triple services, that is, telephone, Internet access, and TV broadcast services.

The advantages of NGN from viewpoints of users are as follows:

(1) More versatile mobility and nomadicity than with the existing cellular phone service. More generalized horizontal and vertical roaming is supported, between fixed and mobile access points, between domestic and international cellular networks, and between any type of wireless access including cellular networks and WLANs.

(2) The triple play services of telephone, Internet access, and TV broadcast services.

(3) Through a single FMC network access arrangement, users can also enjoy broadband and ubiquitous services. Ubiquitous services provide relevant content and information delivery to users wherever they are.

(4) NGN provides networking and interconnection of ubiquitous devices in appliances such as refrigerators, television sets, vehicles, garage doors for remote sensing and controlling. Such applications will build a new large market.

4   NGN

4.1   NGN as a Target Network

As a target network, the followings were defined to identify and specify NGN to be standardized in ITU.

(1) NGN is a packet-based network providing telecommunication services.
(2) It makes use of multiple broadband, QoS-enabled transport technologies.

(3) Service-related functions are independent from underlying transport-related technologies.

(4) It provides unfettered access for users to networks and to competing service providers and/or services of their choice.

(5) It supports generalized mobility, allowing consistent and ubiquitous provision of services to users.

It is to be noted that item (3) above is essential to build secure NGN.   The flexibility of Internet Protocol was the key for the rapid penetration of the Internet.   On the other hand, such flexibility is too flexible and is misused by ill-will users, who intentionally try to damage the Internet or its users by attacking or sending malware or viruses. The separation will make the situation more secure.

Item (4) is also important, which will guarantee that NGN can be installed under any regulations posed depending on countries.

4.2   NGN Architecture

With NGN target defined above, the architecture and interfaces are specified. The IP technology is adopted as NGN core transport technology. To facilitate QoS management in NGN, IP packet transport- and service-related functions are clearly separated as shown in Figure 5. [9]

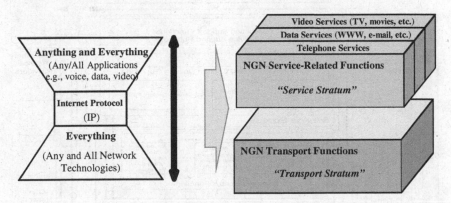

Fig. 5. Next Generation Networks -Principles-

A group of transport-related functions is named 'transport stratum', and a group of the service related function is named 'service stratum'. The terminology 'stratum' is adopted in order to avoid any confusion with the "layers" defined in the Open Systems Interconnection (OSI) model. Transport layer functions are limited to the OSI lower layer functions. But, the transport stratum could include OSI higher layer functions in heterogeneous network environments. The NGN architecture is shown in Figure 6 [10].

4.3   NGN Interfaces

In NGN, four types of interfaces are defined, User-Network Interface (UNI), Network-to-Network Interface (NNI), Application Network Interface (ANI) and Service Network Interface (SNI). ANI and SNI are newly defined and are very specific to NGN. They are defined to provide interfaces to promote interactions with application providers and service providers. Traditionally they used to be interconnected to networks with UNI as users.

ANI (application network interface) is the interface with other service providers and their applications, or application providers. It supports control plane level type of interaction without media (data) level interaction. NGN operators can be application providers

SNI (service network interface) is the interface with other service providers, such as content providers. It supports both control plane level type of interactions and media (data) level type of interactions.

The specific difference between application providers and service providers, i.e., the difference between ANI and SNI is the media (date) interaction. Service providers support a complete set of services, whereas application providers support control functions associated with the enhanced applications.

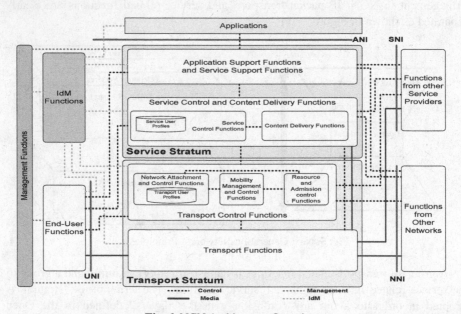

Fig. 6. NGN Architecture Overview

4.4   NGN and Intelligent Networks

The separation of transport stratum and service stratum is similar to the concept of separation of transport functions and service control functions in Intelligent Network (IN).

IN were developed for quick provisioning of supplementary services in telephone networks by separating basic transport functions and service control functions. IN deploys the common channel signaling network for signaling transport between switching systems. Switching controls are achieved by the service control point (SCP). Each switching system is dedicated to the simple switching functionality as a service switching point (SSP) under the control of a common SCP. The basic configuration of the intelligent networks is shown in Figure 7.

The separation of the two functional groups enables quick and easy service creation and service provisioning by adding/modifying service software to the SCP, which is shared among all SSPs. This was not the case in traditional telephone network where a new service deployment would require changes to all related switching systems.

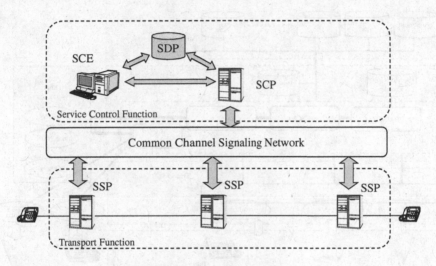

SSP: Service Switching Point (SSP)
SDP: Service Data Point (SDP)
SCP: Service Control Point
SCE: Service Creation Environment

Fig. 7. Basic Configuration of Intelligent Network

The toll-free dial service, for example, requires translation of the dialed number to/from the regular subscriber telephone number as a service control function at SCP.

The simple addition of that translation function to SCP enables a new toll-free dial service on a nation-wide basis.

4.5   IMS-Based NGN Configuration [7]

NGN is implemented using the IP Multimedia Subsystem (IMS) that the 3GPP (3rd Generation Partnership Project) has developed for multimedia communication with the third generation cellular technology [11, 12]. The IMS-based NGN deploys the IMS accommodating NGN architecture and requirements such as FMC.

The IMS core consists of three types of SIP (Session Initiation Protocol, RFC3261) servers at the service stratum to carry out the following functions: CSCF (Call Session Control Function), S-CSCF (Serving-Call Session Control Function), I-CSCF (Interrogating-Call Session Control Function), and P-CSCF (Proxy-Call Session Control Function), as shown in Figure 8.

The S-CSCF SIP server is the primary server providing user authentication and relaying messages to application servers. The I-CSCF SIP server receives SIP registration messages from the P-CSCF SIP server and reroute the massages to the appropriate S-CSCF SIP server. Finally, the P-CSCF SIP server is the primary server, which directly contacts user terminals.

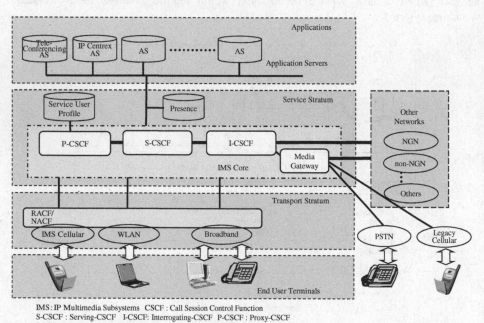

IMS: IP Multimedia Subsystems CSCF : Call Session Control Function
S-CSCF : Serving-CSCF I-CSCF: Interrogating-CSCF P-CSCF : Proxy-CSCF
RACF: Resource and Admission Function, PSTN: Public Switched Telephone Network

Fig. 8. IMS-based NGN Configuration Example

4.6   NGN Services

NGN services are classified as Release 1 Services and Release 2 and after Services. The list of services available in NGN Release 1 is given in Table 1, which includes all existing telecommunication and Internet services such as multimedia services, PSTN/ISDN, emulation/simulation services, Internet access, and public interests. The NGN release 1 Services are equivalent to services which are provided by telecom networks and the Internet, as shown in Table 1. As the next generation carrier grade network, NGN should support services of public interests, such as emergency calls and lawful interception in addition to POTS/ISDN emulation and simulation.

NGN services supported by NTT's NGN based on ITU-T NGN Release 1 services as of end of March 2008 are summarized in Table 2 [13-15].

Table 1. NGN Release 1 Service Capabilities

Service Type	Outline
Multimedia Service	Real-time conversational voice services
	Real-time text
	Presence and general notification services
	Messaging service
	Push to talk
	Point-to-Point interactive multimedia services (video telephony)
	Collaborative interactive communication services
	Content delivery services
	Push-based services
	Broadcast/multicast services
	Hosted and transit services for enterprises (e.g., IP Centrex)
	Information services (e.g., highway monitoring)
	VPN services
	3GPP release 6 and 3GPP2 release A OSA-based services
PSTN/ISDN Emulation	Same or better PSTN/ISDN service
PSTN/ISDN Simulation	PSTN/ISDN like service
Internet Access	Legacy Internet Access
Other Services	VPN
	Data retrieval (e.g., tele-software)
	Data Communications (e.g., file transfer, Web browsing)
	On-Line applications (e.g., On-line marketing, e-commerce)
	Sensor network service
	Remote Control/tele-action(e.g., Home application control, telemetry, alarming)
	OTN (Over-the-Network) device management
Public Interests	Lawful interception
	Malicious communication identification
	Emergency telecommunication
	User identifier presentation and privacy
	Network or service provider selection
	Support of users with disabilities
	Number portability
	Service unbundling
	Unsolicited bulk telecommunications protection

Table 2. NGN Commercial Services in Japan

Service		Content
Optical Broadband service (FLET'S Hikari Next service)		Service for Residential Users (single family house)
		Service for Residential Users (apartment house)
		Service for Business users
Optical Telephony service(Hikari Denwa and Hikari Denwa Office Type)	QoS Guaranteed	Hikari Telephony (Standard QoS, High QoS: 7kHz)
		Business Telephony
		Video Telephony
VPN service (FLET'S VPN Gate service)	QoS Guaranteed	VPN (Center-to-end, CUG) To be provided
	Best Effort	VPN (Center-to-End, CUG)
Content Delivery Service (FLET'S Cast service)	QoS Guaranteed	Unicast
		Multicast
	Best Effort	Unicast
		Multicast
Ethernet over NGN (Business Ether Wide service)		Ethernet

5   NGN Issues

5.1   IPv6 Issues

IPv6 is specified to be allowed multi-homing arrangements. [RFC2460] When an end-host is connected to more than one Internet service provider (ISP) with more than one interface, the arrangement is referred to as multihoming. The primary objective is to increase the quality and robustness of the connection.

NGN provide interconnection to the Internet as a service menu as designed. The IPv6 address is naturally suitable as addressing in NGN. In case of Internet connection through NGN, an NGN terminal is given NGN IPv6 by NGN and ISP IPv6 by ISP. NGN IPv6 address is used for routing in NGN to the ISP, but the connection to ISP requires ISP IPv6 address. By using ISP IPv6 address, NGN cannot deal with the address for routing in NGN. (see Figure 9)

The suggested solutions are as follows:

(1) Native NGN IPv6 addressing is used for end terminals, or

(2) Tunneling functions are equipped to go through NGN for the connection to ISP by using ISP IPv6 addressing.

The first solution is the simplest, but it will be difficult for ISPs which already allocated their IPv6 addresses to their users before NGN.

The issue for the second solution is whether tunneling function should be equipped in NGN side or ISP side. Total number of ISPs will be more than thousands. Therefore, it is not economical to equip more than thousands of tunneling functions in NGN, each of which interfaces each ISP independently. On the other hand, some ISPs are not big enough to invest on tunneling functions with no expectation for additional value. Harmonized solutions are to be sought.

In Japan, three big representative ISPs were chosen and three tunneling functions are equipped in NGN toward these three ISPs. Other ISPs will be connected through three representative ISPs.

Another IPv6 issue is Web access under IPv4 and IPv6 coexistence environments. When an ISP without IPv6 capabilities is requested by an IPv6 end host, the fallback to IPv4 requires 20 seconds, i.e., more than 20 seconds delay for connection establishment. This will not be completely resolved until full IPv6 penetration.

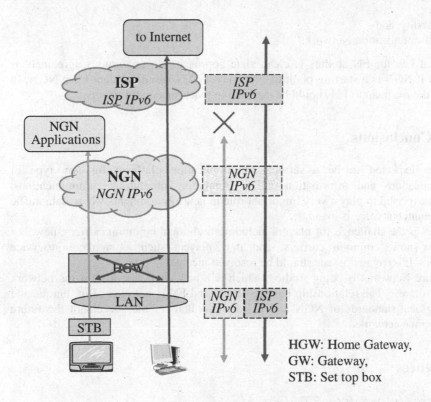

HGW: Home Gateway,
GW: Gateway,
STB: Set top box

Fig. 9. IPv6 Multi-prefix Issues

5.2   Traffic Offload

Data bits produced in smartphones is more than 30 times higher than the feature phones. The estimated composite annual growth rate over 2011 and 2016 is 78 %, which will result in 18-fold increase in 2016 over 2011.

Globally, 33 percent of handset and tablet traffic was offloaded onto the fixed network through dual-mode or femtocell in 2011. [5]

NGN provides FMC. It should also take into account such enormous mobile data traffic growth.

5.3   Relationship with Future Networks

ITU-T initiated studies on Future Networks (FN), which is expected to be next to NGN or Future Internet. The identified core areas are [16]

(1) Network Virtualization,
(2) Data-centric Network,
(3) Energy Saving of Networks,
(4) In-system Network Management,
(5) ID,
(6) Mobility, and
(7) Self-optimization Network.

The vital key for FN studies is clean slate approach. No unanimous agreement is reached if NGN is a starting point of FN study, or FN is independent from NGN. In reality, the roadmap to FN should be clarified to reach successful results.

6   Conclusions

NGN is expected to be a service and application platform for any type of communications and information delivery including ubiquitous communications. NGN is expected to play a very important role in new environments where data traffic is dominant, but voice is mandate.

NGN is the challenge for players including traditional common carriers, new, but not new now, common carriers, and new players such as application/service providers. IPv6 related issues should be resolved nicely.

Future Networks is being studied, which is a new challenge toward the network for the future.   The relationship between NGN and FN is not clear. But, unique and single global standards of NGN and FN are essential for the success of the future carrier grade networks.

References

1. http://gigaom.com/2010/03/24/
   mobile-milestone-data-surpasses-voice-traffic/ .
2. Cisco Visual Networking Index (VNI) Global Mobile Data Forecast
3. ITU, Measuring the Information Society 2012, ITU (2012)
4. Internet World Stats (2012), http://www.internetworldstats.com/
5. Cisco VNI,
   http://www.cisco.com/en/US/solutions/collateral/ns341/ns525/
   ns537/ns705/ns827/white_paper_c11-520862.html

6. FCC/DA 251763, Report and Order FCC 04-188 (Adopted August 4, 2004) (Released August 19, 2004)
7. Asatani, K.: Next Generation Networks (NGN) in Enterprises. In: Handbook of Enterprise Integration, ch. 5. Taylor and Francis, London (November 2009)
8. Saltzer, J.H., Reed, D.P., Clark, D.D.: End-to-end arguments in system design. ACM Trans. Comput. Syst. 2(4), 277–288 (1984)
9. ITU-T Recommendation Y.2011, General Principles and General Reference Model for Next Generation Network, Geneva (October 2004),
   http://www.itu.int/publications
10. ITU-T Recommendation Y.2012, Functional Requirements and Architecture of the NGN Release 1, Geneva (September 2006), http://www.itu.int/publications
11. Camarillo, G., Garcia-Martin, M.-A.: The 3G IP Multimedia Subsystem (IMS): Merging the Internet and the Cellular Worlds, 2nd edn., ch. 3. John Wiley & Sons, New York (2006)
12. ITU-T Recommendation Y.2021, IMS for Next Generation Networks (September 2006), http://www.itu.int/publications
13. NTT, Interface for IP network service (data communications) on Next Generation Network v.1, NTT Technical reference (2007) (in Japanese)
14. NTT, Interface for IP network service (voice communications) on Next Generation Network v.1, NTT Technical reference (2007) (in Japanese)
15. NTT, Interface for IP network service (LAN type communications) on Next Generation Network v.1, NTT Technical reference (2007) (in Japanese)
16. ITU-T Recommendation Y.3001, Future Networks - Objectives and Design Goals (May 2011)

A Rendezvous Mobile Broker for Pub/Sub Networks

Augusto Morales Dominguez, Tomas Robles, Ramon Alcarria, and Edwin Cedeño

Technical University of Madrid,
Av. Complutense 30. Madrid, Spain
{amorales,trobles,ralcarria,edwinc}@dit.upm.es

Abstract. On the current Internet, Publish/Subscribe (Pub/Sub) systems are gaining popularity as efficient, simple, and scalable communication mechanisms. Mobile Pub/Sub systems are the next step for distributed Pub/Sub networks. On the other hand, the constrained characteristics of mobile nodes can limit the subscription expressiveness of the content consumers, and the overlaying applications and services. This paper describes a mobile broker model, that we call Rendezvous Mobile Broker, for integrating mobile nodes as fully-functional brokers. RMBs can delegate Pub/Sub tasks to other brokers and extend the subscription expressiveness in runtime; so, this delegation improves the mobile Pub/Sub systems' suitability for scenarios with multiple content types.. This paper also describes a subscription allocation algorithm for extending the amount of subscriptions the mobile broker supports, in the form of topic-based subscriptions. Finally, we describe a proof of concept and validate the algorithms using real devices.

Keywords: Publish/Subscribe system, mobile brokers, subscription algorithm.

1   Introduction

It is a fact that today's networks are composed of both fixed and mobile devices that share content without having a real concern about the source of the information as long as they can consume it. In this context, the Publish/Subscribe (Pub/Sub) paradigm [2] has emerged as an attractive communication model because of its asynchronous, time and process decoupled style. On the current Internet, the Pub/Sub systems have been successfully extended to content dissemination services such as: PubSubHubbub [4] and XMPP [3], as well as they have being considered as a promising communication model for Future Internet architectures [8]. In addition, it has supported content consumption, especially when information producers and consumers are limited by mobile devices' constrains, such as: low processing power, battery and storage.

Publish/Subscribe systems, which are also knows as event-based systems, are basically composed of three main components [2]: publishers which are the content producers, subscribers that express their willingness to consume specific content; and finally brokers that put in contact publishers and subscribers by storing and forwarding this information. Depending on the scenario, mobile devices can perform as publishers or subscribers; so their capability of consuming or publishing content

J. Lloret Mauri and J.J.P.C. Rodrigues (Eds.): GreeNets 2012, LNICST 113, pp. 16–27, 2013.
© Institute for Computer Sciences, Social Informatics and Telecommunications Engineering 2013

depends on the expressiveness [2] of the subscription language of the Pub/Sub network.

Pub/Sub systems are quite common in large-scale networks and infrastructures, where brokers have enough processing power to put in contact content producers and subscribers; so Pub/Sub brokers control [2] the Subscriptions' states, the Event Routing, and finally the Matching Process. In this context, there are many algorithms [10] and mechanisms [5] for optimizing their Pub/Sub systems. Pub/Sub systems have also proven their advantages [19] [21] regarding flexibility and integration with other layers. Despite this, these scenarios are not as restricted as mobile computing scenarios where resources are constrained and content dissemination strategies [12] are not applicable. Hence, there are still challenges for integrating mobile devices as fully-functional elements [9] capable of carrying out energy-efficient tasks in distributed Pub/Sub scenarios. This integration is one of the targets of future ubiquitous computing scenarios [1] [20], where multiple participants in Pub/Sub networks might be consuming/publishing information, through standardized interfaces (e.g. the OMA interfaces [6]). In the same way, mobile participants will be able to extend their nearby environments (e.g. PAN and WSN networks) to the same Pub/Sub networks. Hence, sooner or later mobile brokers will be fully-integrated with local and fixed Pub/Sub infrastructures as one single content dissemination network together with external brokers and Pub/Sub network clouds.

In this paper, we describe models to integrate mobile devices as Pub/Sub brokers and propose delegation mechanism with fixed Pub/Sub infrastructures. Therefore, we introduce the concept of Rendezvous Mobile Broker (RMB) which integrates resource control techniques that improve the subscription management cost and a novel coordination model focused on mobile Pub/Sub systems. The structure of the paper is as follows. In the first part of section 2 we justify the advantages of mobile brokers over fixed ones in some situations. As there are many possible scenarios we have focused on a distributed service scenario. Next, we describe our overall Pub/Sub system model. Section 3 introduces the RMB internal model and our strategies for optimizing the model. Next, we describe details of the proof of concept and finally we validate the proposed algorithms.

2   Pub/Sub System Model for Mobile Environments

Nowadays, one of challenges of mobile nodes refers to their integration with distributed content networks. Most of these scenarios are currently supported by a fixed infrastructure of servers, in the form of content dissemination networks, Pub/Sub clouds and so on. Nevertheless, even when mobile nodes consume most of the available content, on the Internet, they are still far of being fully integrated with these networks. This situation lets mobile devices in the first plane of information consumption, but in a second plane on content dissemination support. A similar situation is expected for the service and application layers, which commonly perform as the end-consumers of content. Therefore, the content dissemination mechanisms in mobile environments directly affect the capabilities of the overlay services, and especially those which involve distributed and decentralized workflows.

2.1   Towards the Pub/Sub Mobile Brokers

Despite of the several available scenarios, in this section we use a Cooperative Mobile Service (CMS) scenario for justifying the importance of the Pub/Sub mobile broker and its advantages over having a fixed broker. Cooperative Mobile Services (CMS) [21] are basically decentralized workflows; so taking as example a highly distributed CMS we can assume that, in some cases, the best way of supporting the content dissemination relies on an event-based network, in the form of a decentralized Pub/Sub network. Thus, these services will fully depend on distributed and fixed brokers. However, if the mobile node needs to ensure the independency of the service, it will have to self-manage its Pub/Sub processes in the content dissemination network; so, in some cases, it will have to perform as a Pub/Sub broker instead of a simple Pub/Sub node (publisher or subscriber). For clarifying our point of view we analyze the following cases.

A mobile broker that supports a CMS exclusively requires, for its execution, information from the node's nearby environment (e.g. similar to smart home network proposed in [25], or a PAN network). Hence, there is no need to publish/consume information to/from the outside, since the publishers are subscribers will be kept internally. Therefore, a broker can control the way events are matched and delivered inside the recently created communication space. It can also create an information scope, for managing all the information in this domain, in a specific time and service state. It is clear that a standard fixed broker could support this kind of scenario; however, the executed service (in the mobile node) will have a less level of service-to-Pub/Sub communication space coordination. This is because, if the same mobile device moves to another domain, and has to consume content from other sources including service states (control plane), it will have to re-initialize both the Pub/Sub primitives and the identification of service events (including control plane). Therefore, having a mobile broker can lead to a better integration from the content dissemination and the CMS, which will be reflected in an improved service coordination and event dissemination in the Pub/Sub network.

In another case, the same CMS, is supported by a single Pub/Sub node (instead of a mobile broker) while uses the standard publish and subscribe primitives. In a case of failure of its entry broker, the mobile node can move to another broker (using one of the existing protocols [26]) and recover all the un-received events. However, if the new broker is unaware of the employed protocol the node could subscribe again, but some control events could be lost, and the CMS can acquire an undetermined service state. On the other hand, if the mobile performs as a mobile Pub/Sub broker, it could obtain the right event by adapting, on-the-fly, its event notification protocol with a more resilience one (e.g. using a Gossip-based solution).

In our RMB model, the subscription storage, the matching process and the event notification process, which traditionally are concentrated in fixed brokers, can be distributed for supporting the previous cases. Thus, even if the mobile node moves to another fixed broker, there is no guarantee of maintaining the same level of distribution; so, in order to support this kind of CMS, it is sometimes convenient to migrate publishers and subscribers together with their mobile serving broker. Therefore our mobile Pub/Sub model targets these scenarios, while remains independent from the overlaying services.

2.2   Overall Model

Our mobile Pub/Sub system model is based on the principle that, not only subscriptions but also control information regarding processes could be seamlessly distributed across the Pub/Sub brokers. This information includes subscription tables, subscription events, publication events and Pub/Sub processes. As any traditional Pub/Sub system, brokers have to match events with subscriptions and, in some cases, send these events to other brokers in the network and the subscription they are currently supporting [16]. Thus, the main feature of our model is the Rendezvous Mobile Broker (RMB) which, aside from integrating all the characteristics of standard brokers, it delegates its Pub/Sub processes and subscription information. These mechanisms aim to minimize the workload of the mobile device, optimize its energy resources, and finally expand its subscription capabilities. Following the classic Rendezvous pattern of Pub/Sub networks, we use this name for highlighting the fact that our RMB is responsible of the events which have been published in its local communication space, and will be forwarded to clients' scopes.

Figure 1 depicts our simplified model, which is composed of, at least, two brokers: the RMB and an infrastructure broker, which can manage a bigger workload due to its fixed nature. The model allows transmitting events among content publishers and subscribers in both the mobile and the fixed side. Content publishers in the RMB side can range from a pulseoximeter connected through a Bluetooth connection to an embedded GPS sensor which publishes location information. It is clear that there are integration issues in these sorts of devices and their functionalities as content producers in a Pub/Sub system model. Despite this, there are works [7] that resolve these issues as well as some of them deal with the problem of data format. Therefore, we define a client, as an edge entity of the Pub/Sub network, regardless of the specific implementation or wrapping method [7]. From the subscriber/producer's side our model leaves the typical primitives [2] *publish(), subscribe(), unsubscribe() and notify()* as simple as possible, and keeps the model complexity in the brokers.

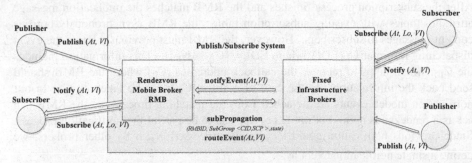

Fig. 1. Overall Pub/Sub System Model

A RMB manages a specific group of clients that may be publishers or subscribers $C_G = \{c_1, c_2, \ldots c_i\}$. Each client c has a unique identifier, a subscription scope S_{CP} which encloses all its subscriptions, and a state C_{st} that keeps a track of the subscription state. Thus, a single client can be expressed as: $c = f(C_{ID}, C_{ST}, S_{CP})$.

2.3   Subscription Model

Regarding the subscription expressiveness [2], the subscription model supports a topic-based and a basic attribute-based subscription. Several trade-offs arise from the subscription expressiveness. If the subscription language is too simple, such as a topic-based one, subscribers shall subscribe to a wide range of events, and then filter themselves their interests. As an example, using the MQTT [22] protocol, if a mobile device requires a sensor output only when its value reaches threshold, it will received all the events regarding this sensor; so later it should have to filter the right value at the application layer. On the other hand, if the broker supports a more sophisticated subscription language (e.g. content-based and type-based), subscribers can issue a tailored subscription and no additional filtering will be needed. Despite this, more complex subscription models increase the complexity of the matching process [15] so they scale better over high capability brokers rather than low–end brokers. We consider mobile devices as low-end brokers, not only because their lower processing power, but also because their energy constrains. Therefore, assuming than most of the events received by a RMB will target local clients, our subscription model focuses on a lightweight subscription model.

A single subscription (S_B) is modeled as a logical or boolean expression applied to a series of attributes (A_T) and its value (V_L). Thus, once the expression (E_x) is enforced to the publication message or event, the subscription is satisfied. Logical expressions include operators such as: "$=,<,>,\neq$". S_B can also represent topic-based interests T_P, so the whole client subscription scope is defined as:

$$S_{CP} = \{\sum_{i}^{n}(A_{Tn}, E_{Xn}, V_{Ln}), \sum_{i}^{n}T_{Pn}\}$$

(1)

2.4   Notification Model

After the subscription process finishes and the RMB matches the publication message attributes/topics with existing subscription tables, the RMB asynchronously notifies content messages to subscribers. However, the RMB must previously know the event dispatching information (EDI), where EDI = $\{C_{ID}, \Delta N_{EV}\}$. This information includes the C_{ID}, which helps to recover the callback addresses (C_B) where the RMB should send back the information. In the case of a single C_B it can be taken as C_{ID}. In our notification model, events are detached from the matching process, so the RMB can act as a rendezvous point, but not necessary has to be part of the notification process. Since previous notification could be already processed $N_{EV}.t$ by other brokers, we define a single notification event as:

$$\Delta N_{EV} = f(C_{ID}, \sum_{i}^{n}(C_{Bn})) - N_{EV}.t$$

(2)

2.5   Process and Coordination Model

There are three types of internal Pub/Sub processes supported by RMB: *the matching process (Mp), event routing (Ep) and notification (Np)*. As the specific clarification of these processes is out of the scope of this article, we focus on how RMBs share information and delegate processes to other fixed brokers. A process $P = \{ID, Exc, Type, State, C_G\}$ ID is the identifier of the RMB that manage the process, *Exc* the broker which currently runs the process. The Types specifies the process role (*Mp, Er, or Np*). *State* defines the state of the process; it can be *Local, Remote,* or *Partial*. Local specifies that the current process is being executed in the RMB. *Remote* denotes that the process is executed outside of the broker. *Partial* indicates that some parts of the process are distributed among the RMB and fixed brokers. As we mention, C_G includes the group of every client supported by a single broker. However, when a broker marks a process as *Partial*, C_G can be split into small groups of clients C_{GT}.

Even when there could be multiple attributes in a single subscription one of the challenges consists of how to organize attributes, values, and topics among the RMB and fixed brokers that participated in the same *Partial* process. Hence, the coordination model establishes and maintains relationships across earlier distributed process using the same Pub/Sub channels. Thus, we extend the definition of a *Partial* process as $P_L = \{T_1, T_2... T_i\}$, where each T_i represents a subtask carried out by a set of brokers. Subtasks perform the same job as the *Mp*, or *Np*. In the case of Mp tasks, each T contains a S_{CP} chunk of a single client, as well as the client identifier it currently supports. We show the overall model in Figure 2.

For the coordination model we assume the processes are already started for a coordinator entity which manages their state. Therefore, the coordinator entity creates (1) a Pub/Sub coordination space (PSC) that is used by inter-process communication. The PSC is location-independent, and can be managed by the RMB or fixed brokers. The coordinator also group tasks (2, 3a, 3b, 3c) by setting identical identifiers for tasks belonging to the same process.

As we previously mentioned, the coordination model is based on Pub/Sub channels. Hence, there could be several internal processes consuming the information at the same time, which offers some sort of redundancy for the entire system. Regarding the event routing, the coordination model is location independent, so it can work on top of existing mechanisms [16]. The PSC encloses a control channel for managing the current state of tasks, and a data channel for content notification, as long as they are subscribed to the same *Partial* Process (4a, 4b). Event Dispatcher tasks must subscribe to content (5a), for allowing matched content (5b) flow from matchers to the event dispatcher (6), and finally to clients. This subscription is also controlled by the coordinator, which can run together with the RMB and enables or disables processes on demand.

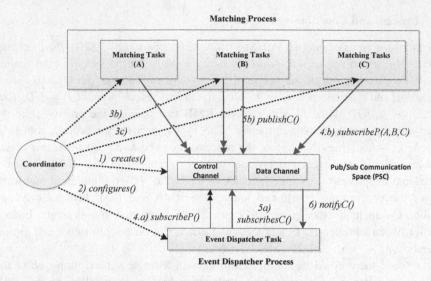

Fig. 2. Control Model for a Partial Process

3   RMB Internal Model

Our model supports topic and attribute-based publish/subscribe. In topic-based subscription, the RMB has to match clients' membership to single topics, which are stored in the form of Counting Bloom Filters [17] (CBF). CBF are a special type of Bloom Filters that allow a space-efficient probabilistic representation of a set that support membership queries and support membership removal

3.1   Subscription Allocation over Brokers

The RMB maintains a single CBF per every topic it has to match, so it stores the clients' subscription that match a single topic in the CBF. This method has more advantages in comparison with storing one single CBF per client, because most of the current topic-basic subscriptions include the notion of recursive subscription. As an example, the MQTT [22] protocol makes use of this sort of subscription in the form of wildcards. In addition, storing subscription in CBF instead of hash tables, or XML representations, does not limit the RMB capability of sharing client's subscription to other brokers, due to the fact that brokers can still map a topic BF with the RMB they are currently serving. Despite this, both RMB and broker must agree with data format and communication protocol. Figure 1 shows the subPropagation (RMB$_{ID}$, SubGroup <C$_{ID}$,S$_{CP}$ >,state) function we have defined for this task; where *state* allows RMB to modify the state (enabled or disabled) of shared CBF among brokers. In the case of attribute-based memberships, the multiple possible values of every subscription's attribute do not allow the same storage strategy of a topic-based subscription. Despite this, we propose our alternative Subscription Allocation Algorithm (SAA), showed in Figure 3, based on the fact that RMB, because their constrained characteristics, only manages light-weighted logical operation (E$_x$), such as: "=" or "≠". Therefore, the RMB can let fixed brokers to carry on remaining complex matching [16] operations.

```
1: procedure Subscription_Arrived (ev)
2:    if ev.TYPE matches A_T then
3:       for each A_T in ev.msg
4:          C.E_x <- getType(A_T)
5:       if ( C.E_x matches (EQUAL) || C.E_x matches (NEQUAL) ) and RMB.STATE
6:             if A_T isElementOf Sub.A_T then
7:                 allocateSub (A_T, C.E_x)
8:             else
8:                 create CBF.A_T
9:                 allocateSub (A_T, C.E_x)
10:          else
11:               assign verifyAvailable (P_L) to P_L.Br_K
12:               invoke subPropagation(RMB_ID, Sub <C_ID,S_cp >,true) for P_L.Br_K
13:    else
14:       if ev.TOPIC isElementOf Sub.T_p
15:          include ev.T_p to Sub.T_p
16:       else
17:          create CBF and include Sub.T_p
1: subprocedure allocatedSub(A_T, C.E_x, ev)
2:    for a C.E_x that matches E_x ∈ currentE_x.Vector
3     VL_ID = hash( A_T.V_L)
4:       if VL_ID isnotElementOf A_Tk.E_xk.CBF_k
5:          σ = create A_Ti.E_xi.CBF_i
6          assign VL_ID to σ and save VL_ID
7:          insert VL_ID in A_Tk.E_xk.CBF_k
8:          insert ev.C_B in A_Ti.E_xi.CBF_i
9:       else
10:         recover A_Ti.E_xi.CBF_i from VL_ID
11:         insert ev.C_B in A_Ti.E_xi.CBF_i
```

Fig. 3. Pseudocode of the Subscription Allocation Algorithm (SAA)

The SAA performs as a attribute-grouping process that condense subscription. The first steps of the SAA algorithm (1-4) extract, from the subscription, the operation associated with the attribute. From 5 to 9, the algorithm determines the sort of logical operation, as well as the existence of the same kind of attribute. In the last case, it allocates the subscription. In the next step, the algorithm checks (11-12) if there are available matching processes that can support the subscription, then it and propagates the subscription over them. The last step saves topic-based subscriptions in the form of CBF. The allocatedSub sub-procedure, matches (1) events with currently supported logical operators. Then, it hashes (3) the attribute value and compares if the value exists in the CBF assigned for the operator and attribute. If the condition is false (4-8) the algorithm creates a new CBF and register C_B in another CBF which points at the new register. The true condition, recovers the CBF using the VL_{ID} and inserts (10,11) the new value.

3.2   Managing Distributed Processes

As we previously mentioned on Section 2.5, the coordinator manages the fragmented processes using a Pub/Sub channel. For this task it employs the Channel Creating Algorithm shown in Figure 4. The subPropagation() function propagates the subscription across fixed brokers. Our model expects that after this process there might be several mechanisms for arranging subscriptions according to their volume, their Pub/Sub language or even the fixed brokers' availability. Hence, the algorithm arranges subscriptions according to predefined group types S_{type} (e.g. high, medium, or default priority). However other complex techniques [15] could be implemented. Even though, we define our own algorithm using publish and subscribe primitives. Thus, let S_B *be* ϵ S_U which is a subscription group and take S_U and S_{type} as our algorithm inputs.

The first (2-3) steps verify previous S_{type} which matches existing Pub/Sub Control Communication Spaces (PSC_k). In the true case, the algorithm publishes the S_U using the corresponding PSC_k identifier. In the other case, the algorithm assigns (5) the suitable tasks' instances to T_{MTi} , T_{EDi} which are Matching and Event dispatching instances respectively. In this assignment, our algorithm defines a nearest neighbor selection method; nevertheless, more sophisticated mechanisms could be adapted. Steps from 6 to 8 create a P_L instance and assign the current PSC_i to it. The invoke actions (9-10) inform T_{Mi} and T_{EDi} to subscribe to the P_L using unique topic-based identifiers ($ID.MT_i$ and $ID.ED_i$), which can be easily managed by the broker of the PSC_k. Finally the algorithm publishes (10) subscriptions and all the event dispatching information C_{IDk} . CB_k needs in order to notify messages to subscribers, through the RMB or directly (e.g. using a web-hook)). Concerning tasks' control, as the coordinator keeps a record of available brokers, it can later update the event notification process by requesting new available ones to subscribe to PSC_k. $ID.ED_k$.

```
1: procedure Channel_Establishment (S_U, S_type)
2:    if S_type. isElement of PSC_k then
3:        publish (PSC_k , S_U)
4:    else
5:        assign getAvailableInstances() to T_Mi , T_EDi
6:            create P_L i = T_Mk + T_EDk.
7:            create new PSC_i = {new ID.MT_i , new ID.ED_i }
8:            assign new PSC_i to P_L i
9:            invoke (T_Mi. subscribeTo({ PSC_i. ID.MT_i }) )
10:           invoke (T_EDI. subscribeTo({ PSC_i. ID.ED_i } ) )
11:           publish (PSC_i. ID.MT_i ,S_U)
12:           publish (PSC_i. ID.ME_i , C_IDk. CB_k ∈ S_U )
```

Fig. 4. Pseudocode of the Channel Creation Algorithm

4   Evaluation

In order to validate our model we have implemented a RMB and the coordination entity. Regarding the implementation of the fixed broker, authors refer to previous works [18], which were modified for supporting the proposed models. We evaluated the scalability of the Subscription Allocation Algorithm for subscription management. We have used a Samsung Nexus S, running OS Android 4.0.4 with a heap size increased from 24 to 48 Mbytes, and the CPU speed overclocked to 1.2 GHz.

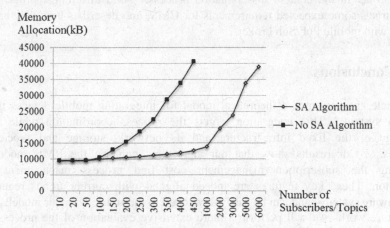

Fig. 5. Evaluation of the SAA implementation

The Y axis of Figure 5 shows the memory allocated by the OS to the RMB instance as the number of subscription/topics increases. The subscription and topics are incremented by the same factor, in order to validate the most demanding scenario. The implementation of the SA algorithm shows that the maximum set of subscriptions threshold starts around 6000 subscribers/topics, while the full-membership store method (based on storing the exact subscription) comes up around 450 subcribers/topics. These results verify the algorithm's feasibility and introduce the subPropagation function threshold for this RMB implementation. Regarding the event-dispatching process time the full-membership storage case performs, in average, slightly better than our subscription storage strategy, 0.180msec versus 0.380msec. This is because the RMB still has to locate the specific C_B addresses. However, the advantages the algorithm offers in term of subscription allocation can overcome this fact in scenarios with multiple subscribers.

5   Related Works

Pub/Sub models and architectures for mobile environments have been previously tackled by works [11] [14]. Nevertheless, they are focused on content dissemination strategies and event mobility. Works such as [12] propose theoretical Pub/Sub models and event distribution strategies, and describe some high level constrains of mobile brokers. Other models [5] integrate mobile brokers in Pub/Sub systems and target the subscriber information delegation, but show neither real nor simulated evaluations. Concerning the integration of Pub/Sub mobile brokers with nearby environments, other works [23] proposed middlewares for unifying the way, mobile brokers publish content. Other researches [24] clarify the advantages of integrating portable Pub/Sub systems with existing human networks, not only with sensors, but also with users' content. Our work explores a different approach by managing Pub/Sub processes and subscription allocation, which affect the capability of the mobile broker in the content dissemination process. As a different approach, our work extracts some expected requirements for CMS, and describes how they can be fulfilled with mobile Pub/Sub brokers.

6   Conclusions

This article has presented a theoretical model for integrating mobile devices into a Pub/Sub system. This integration targets the process coordination while takes advantage of the fixed infrastructure and its network, storage and processing resources. Our results show that our algorithms enhance the RMB model by improving the subscription management cost and process management and distribution. These key features are indeed aligned with current trends regarding energy aware systems, and can be easily developed in the future with our model.

In future works we will perform a more extensive evaluation of the process and coordination model including the SAA algorithm. We will also address the matching-delay issues for systems with high amount of subscriptions. We are also actively exploring the benefits of changing the Pub/Sub notification process (from RMB to fixed brokers) on-the-fly, especially for highly distributed service scenarios with larger numbers of subscribers, using the ns-3.

Acknowledgments. This work is supported by project CALISTA TEC2012-32457. We would like to thank to the School of Telecommunication Engineering (ETSIT).

References

1. Future Internet Core Platform. FI-WARE High Level Description,
   http://www.fi-ware.eu/our-vision/
2. Eugster, P., Felber, P., Guerraqui, R., Kermarrec, A.: The many faces of publish/subscribe. ACM Computing Surveys (2003)
3. IETF RFC 6120. The Extensible Messaging and Presence Protocol (XMPP)
4. Pubsubhubbub project homepage,
   http://code.google.com/p/pubsubhubbub/
5. Kiani, S.L., Knappmeyery, M., Baker, N., Moltchanov, B.: A Federated Broker Architecture for Large Scale Context Dissemination. In: IEEE 10th International Conference Computer and Information Technology (2010)
6. OMA Next Generation Services Interface V1.0. NGSI-10
7. Alcarria, R., Robles Valladares, T., Morales Domínguez, A., López-de-Ipiña, D., Aguilera, U.: Enabling Flexible and Continuous Capability Invocation in Mobile Prosumer Environments. SENSORS 12, 8930–8954 (2012)
8. Pursuit FP7 –EU Project, http://www.fp7-pursuit.eu/PursuitWeb/
9. Muhl, G., Ulbrich, A., Herrman, K.: Disseminating information to mobile clients using publish-subscribe. IEEE Internet Computing 8(3), 46–53 (2004)

10. Martins, J.L., Duarte, S.: Routing algorithms for content-based publish/subscribe systems. IEEE Communications Surveys & Tutorials 12(1) (2010)
11. Rezende, G., Rocha, B.P.S., Antonio, A.: Publish/subscribe architecture for mobile ad hoc networks. In: ACM Symposium on Applied Computing (2008)
12. Huang, Y., Garcia-Molina, H.: Publish/subscribe in a mobile environment. Journal of Wireless Network 10(6) (2004)
13. Ouksel, A.M., Lundquist, D.: Demand-driven publish/subscribe in mobile environments. Journal of Wireless Network 16(8) (2010)
14. Salvador, Z., Alzua, A., Larrea, M., Lafuente, A.: Mobile XSiena: towards mobile publish/subscribe. In: ACM International Conference on Distributed Event-Based Systems (2010)
15. Li, M., Ye, F., Kim, M., Chen, H., Lei, H.: Scalable and Elastic Publish/Subscribe Service. In: IEEE International Parallel & Distributed Processing Symposium (2011)
16. Kazemzadeh, R.S., Jacobsen, H.A.: Partition-Tolerant Distributed Publish/Subscribe Systems. In: 30th IEEE Symposium on Reliable Distributed Systems, October 4-7, pp. 101–110 (2011)
17. Broder, A.: Network applications of bloom filters: A survey. Internet Mathematics 1 (2002)
18. Morales Domínguez, A., Novo, O., Wong, W., Alcarria, R.: Towards the Evolution of PubSub Internetworking Mechanisms with PSIRP. International Journal of Computer Information Systems and Industrial Management Applications 5, 050–059 (2012)
19. Hobbert, J., Mack, D., Schmidt, D.: Integrating Machine Learning Techniques to Adapt Protocols for QoS-enabled Distributed Real-time and Embedded Publish/Subscribe Middleware. Network Protocols and Algorithms 2(3) (2010)
20. Kanjo, E.: Tools and Architectural support for Mobile Phones based Crowd Control Systems. Network Protocols and Algorithm 4(3) (2012)
21. Alcarria, R., Robles, T., Morales Dominguez, A., Cedeno, E.: Resolving Coordination Challenges in Cooperative Mobile Services. In: Sixth International Conference Innovative Mobile and Internet Services in Ubiquitous Computing (IMIS), pp. 823–828 (2012)
22. MQTT Protocol Specificacion v3.1, http://public.dhe.ibm.com/software/dw/webservices/ws-mqtt/mqtt-v3r1.html
23. Tong, X., Ngai, E.C.-H.: A Ubiquitous Publish/Subscribe Platform for Wireless Sensor Networks with Mobile Mules. In: IEEE 8th International Conference on Distributed Computing in Sensor Systems, pp. 99–108 (2012)
24. Zhao, Y., Wu, J.: ZigZag: A Content-Based Publish/Subscribe Architecture for Human Networks. In: 20th International Conference on Computer Communications and Networks, pp. 1–6 (2011)
25. Baladron, C., Aguiar, J.M., Calavia, L., Carro, B., Sanchez, A., Cadenas, A.: User-oriented environment for management of convergent services. IEEE Communications Magazine 50(11), 142–149 (2012)
26. Salvador, Z., Larrea, M., Lafuente, A.: Phoenix: A Protocol for Seamless Client Mobility in Publish/Subscribe. In: 11th IEEE International Symposium on Network Computing and Applications (NCA) (2012)

Router Power Consumption Analysis:
Towards Green Communications

Sebastián Andrade-Morelli, Eduardo Ruiz-Sánchez, Sandra Sendra, and Jaime Lloret

Universidad Politécnica de Valencia,
Camino Vera s/n, 46022, Valencia, Spain
{seanmo,edruisan}@epsg.upv.es, sansenco@posgrado.upv.es,
jlloret@dcom.upv.es

Abstract. In recent years, the number of network devices which are being used in new network infrastructure and intelligent buildings, are growing more and more. Because these devices can often have high processing activity, we must consider their power consumption. Their energy requirements may vary depending on their operation mode, their processing capacity and even the type of devices to which are connected. The ability to determine exact consumption of network can provide an optimal network design and the other auxiliary systems, such as cool system, which may be necessary for the proper operation of the network. In this paper we determine the power consumption generated by network devices of different manufacturers and models. These tests allow us to see the energy consumed when they are in await mode and when they are working, running a routing protocol in order to interconnect different networks, promoting the development of the sustainable Green Networks.

Keywords: Power Consumption, Routers, Switches, Green Networks.

1 Introduction

The increase of mobile devices and the advancement of new technologies, with the possibility to access data networks and Internet, have led us to increase the network infrastructure.

In recent years, there has been an increment of the number of smart phones [1], capable to access to Internet through mobile phone network through wireless access to public networks in cities and public places, which offer this service, improving customer convenience. The implementation of new network services such as data, IP Telephony, IPTV, etc. [2], has also generated the need to increase the number of network devices such as switches and routers. As a consequence of this increment, it has had an increment of the energy consumption in the entire system. We should note that the network devices work better within a temperature range. The range specified by manufacturers is usually between 0-40 °C [3, 4], but the exact value of the operating temperature may change depending on the device or even the task that is running. This factor is important, because the cooling systems must be designed taking into account the correct operating temperature of the devices. A ventilation system should cool a system that generates much heat, should be more powerful, which will mean higher energy consumption.

J. Lloret Mauri and J.J.P.C. Rodrigues (Eds.): GreeNets 2012, LNICST 113, pp. 28–37, 2013.

Given these facts, the energy saving is vital when trying to implement sustainable networks, where the network must never die [5].

Currently, new energy solutions based on the introduction of IP transmission protocol to all areas of the network are being implemented. The migration of these systems to the next generation networks (NGN) generates a saving energy between 30 and 40% [6]. Furthermore, the incorporation of routing systems and IP switching improve the energy efficiency of data transmission networks and voice transmission, where there has been a reduction of the requirements of the network capacity between 60 and 70% [6]. Although other systems such as energy-aware routing protocols, that are being employed in other research fields like in Mobile Ad-hoc Networks [7]), or traffic control systems, to improve the performance [8], we really think that the best way to reduce the energy consumption is to take care of what is being configured in the network devices.

In this paper, we intend to measure the energy consumption of several network routers, depending on its operation mode and the routing protocol that is running (each routing protocol has specific operation features) [9]. In addition, we want to check, if the amount of heat generated by each device is directly related to the device activity. These measures will provide a highly reliable tool for the optimal design of networks and the choice of the most appropriated routing protocol.

The rest of paper is structured as follows. Section 2 presents some previous work and researches regarding to consumption estimation and saving energy in network devices. To perform our tests, we have mounted a network topology, consisting of various network devices. Section 3 shows the topology and characteristics of the used devices. In Section 4 we show the obtained measures from the different tests. Finally, conclusions and future work will be shown in Section 5.

2 Related Works

There is great interest in the analysis of the energy consumption of network devices because the excessive consumption can lead to unexpected and rapid failure of the network.

In [10], S. Sendra et al. presented a survey on power saving techniques and energy issues in wireless sensor networks. They also performed a comparison of several routing protocols and MAC protocols to be used in ad-hoc networks (taking into account their energy constraints).

Other authors have focused their analysis on the energy consumption from the point of view of the development of software tools. These tools aim to help in the control of the consumption of our networks as it is the case of those programmed applications for estimating power consumption of network devices such as routers, switches, etc. The report published in November of 2011 [11] shows a comparative of applications that estimate the power consumption of devices. However, the document indicates that the results provided by this software are not very accurate (they compare their values with the ones gathered from the real power consumption). Therefore, we must understand these tools as approximation tools, that can help us to do an initial design of our system, but they can never replace actual measurements over real devices.

Due to the recent emergence of new network services and applications, networks are growing, regarding to the number of devices. The increase of the number of network devices also implies an increment of the power consumption. In 2009, M. Kakemizu et al. [12] discuss the possibility of keeping the energy consumption in 2025 at the same level as nowadays by reducing the number of equipments and network devices. To do this, authors propose the development of new technologies based on the flow of information going through the network. They propose two mechanisms that allow efficient use of resources. These are called ECO switching and ECO routing. The first one is based on a new model of switching packets that eliminates the packet buffers and routing tables. The second mechanism includes some paths to the routers when the traffic volume is low. This permits them to wait in sleep mode while they do not receive/transmit anything. When a router needs transmit/receive something, it is activated.

Finally, A. P. Bianzino et al. [13] surveyed several strategies to bring the network to the concept of "Green Network" and explained why it is important to close networks to this concept. Authors explain several strategies that would achieve the objectives pursued by a green network. The authors argue that the design strategies should be based on the simplification and unification of the network to avoid excessive network devices. They also propose the implementation of mechanism of selective connection, where routers can turn-off / turn-on depending on their use, and the group of multiple processes and services using virtualization in the same hardware. This is proposed because a single device working at full capacity, consumes less power than several devices running process less complex.

3   Scenario and Hardware Description

In order to perform our measurements, we need to test the performance of several routers from different brands and models. In this section we will see the used routers and their characteristics. To determine the consumption, we have used an electronic device, called "Kill a Watt". The device is able to provide direct measurements of voltage, power and current, without the need for further calculations. The power consumption is given with an accuracy of 1% (0.2W). The section also describes the used topology and the study cases used to take measurements.

To carry out the measures, we used a network topology consisting of four routers, two switches and four computers. Fig. 1 shows the topology used for our purpose. As we can see, the routers are responsible for splitting the networks.

Static routing protocols are often used for small networks, where there are no redundant paths and where there is only one point of attachment to the rest of the network. A dynamic routing protocol is used, if any of the aforementioned conditions is not met. Dynamic routing protocols, allow routers to exchange information. From this information, a router can modify and update their routing tables. In our tests, we have used static routing and the two dynamic routing protocols most used [14]: Routing Information Protocol V.2 (RIP V.2) and Open Shortest Path First (OSPF). In each case, we measured the energy consumption of each network device, when devices are in idle state and while it is executing the routing protocol.

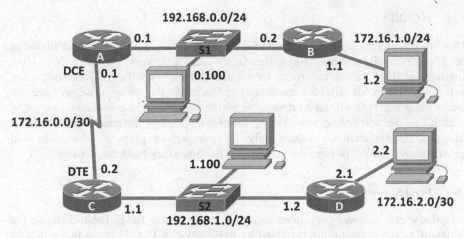

Fig. 1. Network topology

Network devices used in our test have been Cisco 2620, Cisco 1700 and Cisco 1841, from Cisco Systems Inc, router AR410 from Allied Telesyn and 3Com OfficeConnect Remote 531 Access Router of 3Com. The switch used to connect the routers is Cisco Catalyst 2950. In this paper we do not measure the energy consumption of the switches because they are measured in another study. The purpose of this paper is to measure and compare only routers. The study cases included in this paper are:

- 1st study case: Router Cisco 1841 and switches Cisco 2950.
- 2nd study case: Router Cisco 2620 and switches Cisco 2950.
- 3rd study case: Router Allied AR410 and switches Cisco 2950.
- 4th study case: Router Cisco1700 and switches Cisco 2950.
- 5th study case: Router 3Com Office Connect Remote 531 Access.

Table 1 shows the hardware characteristics of each device. All routers allow the static routing protocol.

Table 1. Hardware features for all devices

	Max Data transfer Rate (Gbps)	Operating Temperature (°C)	Internal memory (KB)	Flash memory (KB)	Processor (one processor)	Routing protocol	Data Transmission protocol
Allied AR410	0.1	0-40	16	8192	Motorola MPC860 50 MHz RISC	RIP & RIP v2, OSPF	Ethernet, Fast Ethernet
Cisco 1841	0.1	0-40	191	62720	Motorola MPC860 50 MHz RISC	RIP & RIP v2, OSPF	Ethernet, Fast Ethernet, serial
Cisco 2620	0.1	0-40	32	8192	Motorola MPC860 50 MHz RISC	RIP & RIP v2, OSPF	Ethernet, Fast Ethernet, Serial
Cisco 1700	0.1	0-40	32	8192	Motorola MPC860 50 MHz RISC	RIP & RIP v2, OSPF	Ethernet, Fast Ethernet, Serial
3COM	0.010	0-40	2048	2048	Motorola MC68360 25MHz	-	Ethernet, Serial, ISDN

4   Results

After configuring the static routing and the 2 routing protocols (if they are available in the router) in all devices, we gathered the measurements obtained. We have summarized these values in several tables and graphs, with the goal of comparing their consumption for different operating conditions. In this section, we will see the results obtained. This will let us determine which set of devices consume less energy. In each case we will only discuss the power consumption of the routers, although we also provide the switches values only for comparison purposes. Switches had approximately 17 W·h power consumption all the time (they have not varied).

4.1   First Study Case

First study case test was performed using the router Cisco 1841. Table 2 shows the values of power consumption provided by these devices. Fig. 2 shows the values of power consumption grouped by the protocol configured in the routers. As Fig. 2 shows, the power consumed by all devices is, in all cases, between 16 and 18 W·h. We also note that the routers A and C have consumption slightly superior than the ones shown by routers B and D. This may be because, the devices A and C, are using the serial interface to communicate between them. In addition, we note that the device configured as DTE, consumes about 4% more power than the DCE device.

Table 2. Results of measurement of 1st case

Device	Power consumption (W·h)					
	A	B	C	D	S1	S2
Idle Mode	16.3	16.2	16.9	17.0	16.9	16.5
RIP Protocol	17.3	16.4	17.8	17.1	17.2	16.8
OSPF Protocol	17.3	16.2	17.8	17.3	17.2	16.7
Static Protocol	17.1	16.1	17.5	17.0	17.1	16.7

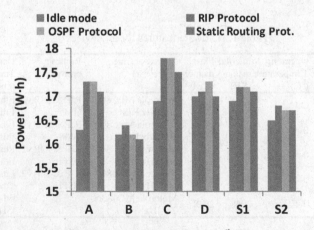

Fig. 2. Power consumption for 1st case

4.2   Second Study Case

Second study case analyzes the behavior of the router Cisco 2620. Table 3 shows the values of power consumption provided by these devices. Fig. 3 shows the power consumption for these devices. In this case, router A and C have around 15 W·h of power consumption, while the power consumption for routers B and D are close to 13.5 W·h. In this case, the difference of power consumption between the routers A/C (with a serial link) and B/D (without a serial link) is around 16%.

Table 3. Results of measurement for 2nd case

Device	Power consumption (W·h)					
	A	B	C	D	S1	S2
Idle Mode	13.8	13.6	14.7	13.3	16.8	16.6
RIP Protocol	14.9	13.7	15.5	13.4	17.2	16.9
OSPF Protocol	15.0	13.6	15.5	13.4	17.2	16.7
Static Protocol	14.8	13.4	15.3	13.3	17.1	16.8

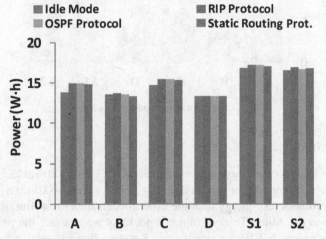

Fig. 3. Power consumption for 2nd case

4.3   Third Study Case

Allied AR410 router presents the lowest power consumption of all devices under this test. Table 4 shows the values of power consumption for this case. If we analyze the consumption of all devices, depending on the protocol they are been running, we can see that all routers have power consumption between 6.5 W·h (for OSPF in router C, configured as DTE) and 6.8 W·h (for RIPV2 in router C, configured as DTE). In idle mode, routers maintain their consumption lower than the 6.6 W·h. These values are shown in Fig. 4.

Table 4. Results of measurement for 3rd case

Device	Power consumption (W·h)					
	A	B	C	D	S1	S2
Idle Mode	6.6	6.4	6.5	6.5	16.8	16.5
RIP Protocol	6.7	6.7	6.8	6.7	17.3	17.1
OSPF Protocol	6.7	6.7	6.5	6.7	17.2	16.9
Static Protocol	6.6	6.5	6.7	6.6	17.2	17.1

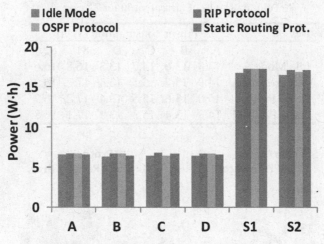

Fig. 4. Power consumption for 3rd case

4.4   Fourth Study Case

The fourth case analyzes the consumption of the router Cisco 1700. Table 5 shows the values of power consumption for this device. Fig 5 shows that this Cisco Systems inc. router model consumes less energy than the other models under test. But, it consumes more energy than the Allied Telesyn router model. As we can see, the protocol that consumes more energy is RIP compared with Static routing protocol, where routers consume around 10 W·h (3% less energy). The router A and C (with the DCE and DTE connection) consume more energy than routers B and D.

Table 5. Results of measurement for 4th case

Device	Power consumption (W·h)					
	A	B	C	D	S1	S2
Idle Mode	9.6	9.2	9.9	9.1	16.7	16.6
RIP Protocol	10.3	9.5	10.8	9.2	17.2	17.1
OSPF Protocol	10.1	9.3	10.6	9.2	17.2	16.9
Static Protocol	9.9	9.0	10.1	8.8	17.1	17.0

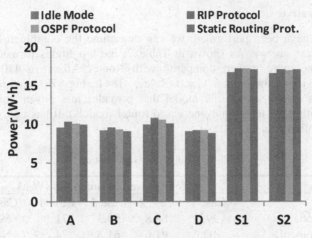

Fig. 5. Power consumption for 4th case

4.5   Fifth Study Case

Finally, we have measured the operation consumption for 3Com Office Connect Remote 531 Access. This model only accepts the static routing protocol. Moreover, the connection between them was using RDSI, so only router A and C was measured. As Table 6 shows, the routers power consumption is around 11.6 W·h. Fig, 6 shows these results in a diagram, where it is easy to see the large difference between the routers and switches consumption.

Table 6. Results of measurement for 5th case

Device	Power consumption (W·h)					
	A	B	C	D	S1	S2
Idle Mode	9.1	-	9.0	-	16.6	16.8
Static Protocol	11.5	-	11.8	-	16.9	17.1

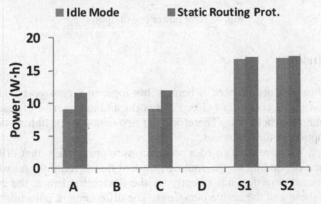

Fig. 6. Power consumption for 5th case

4.6   Comparative

Once the tests have been performed, we can determine the combination of devices that consume less energy. As shown in Table 7, the topologies formed with Cisco routers consume more power, compared with Router Allied AR410, which can consume 40% less power than Cisco Router 1841. Fig. 7 shows these results graphically. As Fig. 7 shows, the model that provides less power consumption is Cisco 1700 (within the three analyzed Cisco router models). It has up to 30% of less power consumption than Cisco 1841.

Table 7. Total power consumption

Device	Total power consumption (W·h)				
	Case 1	Case 2	Case 3	Case 4	Case 5
Idle Mode	99.8	88.8	59.3	71.1	69.7
RIP Protocol	102.6	91.6	61.3	74.1	N/A
OSPF Protocol	102.5	91.4	60.7	73.3	N/A
Static Protocol	101.5	90.7	60.7	71.9	79.4

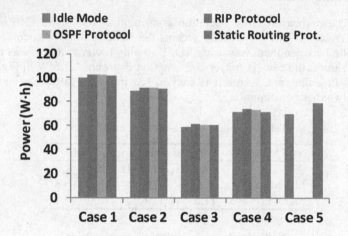

Fig. 7. Total power consumption

5   Conclusion

Saving energy in network devices is being a hot topic in recent years. This is due to the proliferation of the concept of Green Networks and the interest of research groups to develop sustainable networks. Therefore, the first step is to be able to determine the power consumption of these devices.

In this paper, we have performed a power consumption study that different router models consume depending on the routing protocol that is running. As we have seen, the energy consumption depends directly on the device hardware, the configuration capabilities of these and the active interfaces. The difference in consumption between a protocol and another one is small, presenting a maximum difference of 2-3%.

The highest values has been obtained for RIP protocol in study case 1 (102.6 W·h), where we had router Cisco 1841, and the lowest one has been the idle mode in study case 3, Allied AR410 router, (59.3 W·h). Despite of what people think, OSPF has being consuming less energy than RIP in all cases.

In future work, we would like to analyze the operating temperature of the devices, in function on the routing protocol. With this new analysis we will can to establish several design rules for the cooling systems that these devices need, in order to maintain the entire system at a suitable temperature. Moreover we will also compare several switch models from different manufacturers.

References

1. Balasubramanian, N., Balasubramanian, A., Venkataraman, A.: Energy Consumption in Mobile Phones: A Measurement Study and Implications for Network Applications. In: Proceedings of the 9th ACM SIGCOMM Conference on Internet Measurement Conference, IMC 2009, Chicago, IL, USA, November 4-6 (2009)
2. Bianco, C., Cucchietti, F., Griffa, G.: Energy consumption trends in the next generation access network - a telco perspective. In: 29th International Telecommunications Energy Conference, INTELEC 2007, Rome, Italy, September 30-October 4 (2007)
3. Datasheet of Router Cisco184, Available at Cisco web site:
   http://www.cisco.com/en/US/prod/collateral/routers/ps5853/
   ps5875/product_data_sheet0900aecd806c4e2a.pdf
4. Datasheet of Router Allied AR410, Available at Alied telesync web site:
   http://www.alliedtelesis.com/media/fount/datasheet/AR410Seri
   es_Datasheet_RevQ.pdf
5. Fisher, W., Suchara, M., Rexford, J.: Greening Backbone Networks: Reducing Energy Consumption by Shutting Off Cables in Bundled Links. In: Proceedings of the First ACM SIGCOMM Workshop on Green Networking, New Delhi, India, August 30 (2010)
6. González, N., Moran, L., Angioleti, J.M., Varela, J.A.: Green IT, ch. 4. Green Telecom Networks. eKISS n°82. Internal publication of Telefónica (2009)
7. Mohsin, A.H., Bakar, K.A., Adekiigbe, A., Ghafoor, K.Z.: A Survey of Energy-aware Routing protocols in Mobile Ad-hoc Networks: Trends and Challenges. Network Protocols and Algorithms 4(2), 82–107 (2012)
8. Duan, Q.: Performance Evaluation on Traffic Control in Combined Input and Cross-point Queuing Switches. Network Protocols and Algorithms 3(4), 18–31 (2011)
9. Sendra, S., Fernández, P.A., Quilez, M.A., Lloret, J.: Study and Performance of Interior Gateway IP routing Protocols. Network Protocols and Algorithms 2(4), 88–117 (2010)
10. Sendra, S., Lloret, J., Garcia, M., Toledo, J.F.: Power saving and energy optimization techniques for Wireless Sensor Networks. J. Commun. Acad. Publ. 6, 439–459 (2011)
11. Cisco Report. Server power calculator analysis: Cisco UCS power calculator and HP power advisor (2011)
12. Kakemizu, M., Chugo, A.: Approaches to Green Networks. Fujitsu Scientific and Technical Journal 45(4), 398–403 (2009)
13. Bianzino, A.P., Chaudet, C., Rossi, D., Rougier, J.-L.: A Survey of Green Networking Research. IEEE Communications Surveys & Tutorials 14(1), 3–20 (2012)
14. Stevens, W.R.: TCP/IP Illustrated. The Protocols (Addison-Wesley Professional Computing Series), vol. 1 (1994)

RDAP: Requested Data Accessibility Protocol in Vehicular Sensor Networks

Mansour Louiza and Moussaoui Samira

Computing Department, University of Sciences and Technology
Houari Boumediene (USTHB), Algeria
{mansour.louiza,moussaoui_samira}@yahoo.fr

Abstract. Vehicular Sensor Networks (VSNs) are an emerging paradigm in vehicular networks. This new technology uses different kind of sensing devices available in new vehicles, to gather information in order to provide safer, efficient and comfort for roads users. One of the VSNs challenges is how to deal with dynamic data collection. This paper proposes a new multi-hop data collection and dissemination scheme based on data replication on VSNs in an urban scenario. The aim of our proposal scheme is to achieve a high accessibility to requested data while maintaining a low level of channel utilization. The simulation results show that this protocol can achieve significant performance benefits.

Keywords: Vehicular Sensor Network, Data Collection, Data Dissemination, Data Replication.

1 Introduction

In a Vehicular Ad hoc NETworks **VANET** [1, 2], vehicles are provided with wireless connectivity equipment to enable communications with roadside base stations and also between vehicles, to achieve safety, driving assistance, and entertainment. A Vehicular Sensor Network **VSN** can be built on top of a VANET by equipping vehicles with sensing devices. Compared to traditional static sensors, a sensor node is not subject to processing, storage, and energy limitations. Moreover, a mobile sensor node improves sensing coverage with low costs. The two primary distinct features of vehicle networks are that i) vehicles can be highly mobile so an intermittent connectivity , and ii) their mobility patterns are more predictable than those of nodes in Mobile Ad hoc NETworks **MANET** [3] due to the constraints imposed by roads, speed limits, and commuting habits. These specific characteristics generate a number of new research challenges (e.g. data dissemination, data aggregation, data collection, security and authentication ...) that need to be addressed for VSNs to be widely deployed. In this work, we focus on one of the most important topics in VSNs: data collection. The typical scale of a VSN over a wide geographic area, the volume of generated data, important mobility of vehicles and the limited bandwidth make it infeasible to adopt traditional sensor network solutions [4]. The challenge is processing queries in this highly mobile environment and avoids broadcast storm

J. Lloret Mauri and J.J.P.C. Rodrigues (Eds.): GreeNets 2012, LNICST 113, pp. 38–46, 2013.

problem [5] to overcome delay, overhead and accuracy. Some approaches have been proposed to deal data collection in VSNs.   In [1], an opportunistic dissemination is used to harvest meta-data. A cluster based approach is used in [6], and in [7] a data replication technique is used. These approaches have some constraints, as they limit their data harvesting schemes on limited area [1], use centralized access point [6] and a high-cost band for communication [2].

We propose a new scheme for disseminating and harvesting data in a VSN using multi-hop communication and data replication. To reduce overhead, our protocol takes advantage of the vehicle's motion by using a communication between vehicles. The aims of our proposition is to satisfy the requesting vehicle (collect a requested data), and make this data available for other future requesting vehicles.

The rest of this paper is organized as follows. Section II presents the related works focused on data dissemination and data collection on VSNs. Section III describes our proposed protocol. The performance evaluation of this protocol is presented in Section IV. Finally, we conclude the paper and give some perspectives to our work in Section V.

2   Related Work

Several dissemination protocols were proposed for VANETs. They could be sorted into two classes: (i) protocols for infotainment services [1] that have constraints related to the bandwidth, and (ii) protocols for emergency services [8] that have end-to-end delay and delivery ratio constraints.

To collect sensed data, a number of models have been widely used in wireless sensor networks [9, 10]. However, these approaches are less efficient in VSNs because of i) the typical scale of a VSN, ii) the volume of generated data, and iii) vehicles mobility.

We can classify Data collection on VSNs into two main categories: (i) Continuous Data Collection Protocols and (ii) Request-Driven Data Collection Protocols. In a Continuous Data Collection Protocol [2, 5, 6], vehicles are used us a source of information: (i) The vehicles send information issued from their on-board sensors to a server (sink) (ii) The server collects the data and treats them (iii) The server disseminates useful information to the interested vehicles. These kinds of protocols are used in monitoring applications like traffic monitoring, Parking management, Pollution monitoring ... In a Request-Driven Data Collection Protocol [1, 7], the data collection process is initialized by sending a Data Collection Request. The Data Collection Request can be sent either by a moving vehicle or a road infrastructure. This kind of protocols is used to collect a specific data in a defined time and area.

CarTel [6] is a mobile sensor computing system designed to collect, process, deliver, and visualize data from sensors located on vehicles. Each CarTel node uses a geographical dissemination to gather data; process sensor readings and delivering them to a central station (portal). CGP (Clustered Gatheatring Protocol) [2] is a cross-layered gathering, dissemination and aggregation protocol, based on a geographical clustering in a hybrid vehicular architecture (V2V and V2I). It collects information from nodes, aggregates them and sends them to a provider via high cost links.

The MDHP (**M**obEyes **D**ata **H**arvesting **P**rotocol) [1] proposes a solution to disseminate and harvest data. Private vehicles (regular nodes) opportunistically and autonomously spread summaries of sensed data. A harvesting protocol is used by police agents (authority nodes) to build a distributed index of the mobile storage of sensed data. This index allows law enforcement agents to querying a huge database without centralization. MDHR (**M**ulti-hop **D**ata **H**arvesting with **R**eplicas in Vehicular Sensor Networks) [7] presents a multi-hop geographic data dissemination method using data replication technique to collect sensor data in VSNs adopting a V2I communication. In MDHR, to achieve the desired data to the requested vehicle, the only way to communicate is between static nodes, so we can consider the environment used like a traditional WSN. In **Road Probing** [5], the Road Side Unit (RSU) initiates the probing process and selects the passing by vehicles as probes to collect traffic and environment information. The selected vehicles sense the desired data and forward it back to the RSU in a multi-hop fashion.

The aim of our proposal is to develop an efficient strategy to collect a required data. By efficient we mean that the process has to be able to collect data, with a low bandwidth communication cost.

In our approach, we try to satisfy a requesting vehicle and offer a high accessibility to the requested data by using data replication. We take advantage of the vehicles' mobility, thus enable a collaborative harvesting by mobile and static sensor nodes.

3   RDAP: Requested Data Accessibility Protocol in VSNs

Currently, some critical issues in VSNs, such as data transmission delay, packets overhead, and network connectivity are not completely solved. The presented protocols have some restrictive assumptions, as they suppose a data collecting schemes to only single-hop or short distance transmissions [18, 19], or use relay stations and cellular communications to support multi-hop collection [2, 6], which can be very costly and complex. However many of reported works are solutions to specific applications. The presented protocols use either a V2V communication [18] which can induce the broadcast storm problem, or a V2I communication [6, 7] which it's scalable but expensive.

RDAP Requested **D**ata **A**ccessibility **P**rotocol is a new scheme for disseminating and collecting data in a VSN using multi-hop communication and data replication. The aim of **RDAP** is to satisfy vehicle's request and also allow accessibility to the data to other potential requesting vehicles.

3.1   Protocol Environment

We consider a hybrid vehicular sensor network using both V2V and V2I communication in an urban area. The ITS (Intelligent Transports Systems) [20] applications aimed by this proposed protocol are general information services that's provides conviviality like recognize the nearby road situation or traffic monitoring.

On this environment, we assume that the IEEE 802.11p standard is used and the nodes are equipped with a GPS device.

3.2   Protocol Overview

In this section, we detailed the proposed protocol from the request transmission to the data reception. The scheme will be divided into four parts: (i) Data Requesting Phase, (ii) Data Delivery Phase (iii) Data Replication Phase, and (iv) Data Sharing Phase (figure 1).

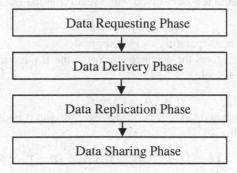

Fig. 1. RDAP phases

   Each node (sensor nodes and vehicular nodes) creates and maintains a neighborhood list via beacon messages, and a received replicas table.

- *Data Requesting Phase*

When a vehicle node needs to collect a data, it sends a request packet. This packet contains vehicle's information (identifier, velocity v (m/s) and coordinates).
Three different cases can be observed:

 - The required data is available on a neighborhood vehicular node: Upon receiving a query, the vehicular node tries to perform it locally in its database. In case of success, the data packet will be automatically sent to the source node. In this phase, the query spreads only because of the vehicle mobility. This communication decreases the packet overhead since there is a probability that another vehicle has before made the same request. After a timeout, if there is no response, the request is sent to a sensor node.

 - The Requested Data is available on a neighborhood static sensor node: In this case this sensor node sends straightforwardly the Data Packet to the vehicular node.

 - The Requested Data is available on a non-neighborhood static sensor node: In this case, the Requested Data is sent to the farthest static node. This static node (**RS**: Requesting Sensor) adds its identifier and its coordinates to the packet, and forwards it. The **RS** initiates a timer "Replication Timer" **RepT** (seconds) which will be used later for supervising the Data Replication process. The value of **RepT** will be the estimated time to retrieve the Data and to deliver it to the **RS** node. The Requested Data will be forwarded, until it reaches the node holding the requested data.

▪ *Data Delivery Phase*

When the node holding the Requested Data receives the Requested Packet, it sends the Requested Data to the previous node on the Requested Packet path.

▪ *Data Replication Phase*

The replication process depends on the requesting vehicle velocity v, the size of the Data p and the sensors transmission rate r. When the **RS** receives the Data, it broadcasts the packet to its neighbors, creating replicas of the Data. For restricting the flooding overhead, we use a Time-To-Live value **TTL**. Equation (1) gives the number of hops that the **RV** has moved while receiving the Data.

$$v \times RepT \div d \tag{1}$$

Where d is the distance separating two sensor nodes.

While equation (2) gives the distance (by hops) the **RV** has traveled while the **Data** is transmitted to the vehicle.

$$v \times (p \div r) \div d \tag{2}$$

The two equations (1) and (2) will be bring together and rounded up to determine the appropriate TTL value.

$$TTL = [v \times RepT \div d + v \times (p \div r) \div d]$$

Depending on the **TTL** value, **RS** broadcasts the Data Packet to its neighbors and sends a unicast message to the farthest static node on the requester vehicular node's direction. This node will do as the **RS** until expiration of the **TTL**. When the **Data** reaches a sensor node close to the initiator vehicular node **RV**, it sends it to the **RV**.

▪ *Data Sharing Phase*

In an urban environment there is a high probability that a number of vehicular nodes request for the same data. In this phase, we use the replicas created in the previous phase. After the replicas are made by a request from the first vehicular node; other following vehicular nodes can benefit from the data availability and access it directly.

4   Performances Evaluation

We evaluate RDAP performance through extensive simulations using ns-2 [21]. For realistic mobility generation, we use SUMO [22] and MOVE [23]. The simulations consider a vehicular network with a number of vehicles between 80 and 120 and 22 sensor nodes distributed uniformly on each side of the road in a 2100*10 m^2 area. The distance between each node is set to 200 m. The average speed of vehicles v is between 0 m/s and 30 m/s and the size of the data p is set to 1000 bytes.

To evaluate the performance, we mainly focused on the number of hops needed to collect the desired data, the transmission delay and the packets overhead.

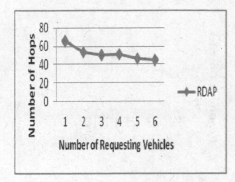

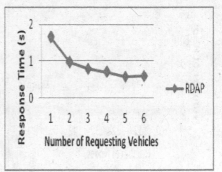

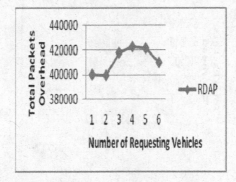

Fig. 2. (a) Number of hops, (b) Response Time, (c) Total Packets Overhead / Number of vehicles requesting for the data

In figure 2, (a), (b) and (c), the x-axis was configured to the number of vehicles requesting for the data, which varies from 1 to 6 (requests number).

Figure 2 (a) shows the number of hops it takes to deliver the requested data depending on the number of requesting vehicles. It can be seen that in the proposed scheme more the number of vehicle requesting the data is important, more the number of hops of data delivery decreases. This is the benefit of data replication, where vehicles can access to the data more easily.

Figure 2 (b) shows the response time to deliver the data from sending the first request packet to receiving the last data packet depending on the number of vehicles requesting the data. It can be seen that more the number of vehicle requesting the data is important, more the delivery time decrease. This is due that vehicles can reach the data more quickly, because of data replication process and communication between vehicles.

Figure 2 (c) shows the total Packet overhead generated by our proposition. We can observe that more the number of vehicles requesting for the data increase, more the packet overhead is important, till it reach the fifth vehicle, where the packet overhead decreases due that the vehicle found the data more quickly cause the data sharing technique used by our proposition reduces further packet overhead, as no replicas are created.

In figure 3, (a), (b) and (c), the x-axis was configured to the number of nodes in the network, which varies from 102 to 142.

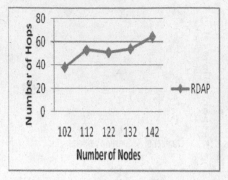
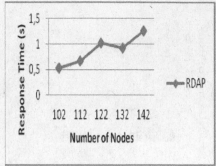

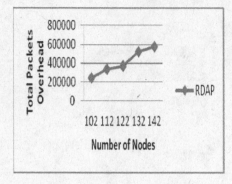

Fig. 3. (a) Number of hops, (b) Response Time, (c) Total Packet Overhead / Number of Nodes

Increase the number of nodes causes more packets exchange in the network, causing collisions. Therefore, in figure 3 (a), we can observe an increase of number of hops in the proposed scheme as the number of nodes increase.
The same results can be seen for the latency in figure 3 (b), where the time of response increases as the number of nodes increase.

Caused by the beaconing messages, the total Packet overhead generated by our proposition increase gradually as the number of nodes increase (figure 3 (c)).

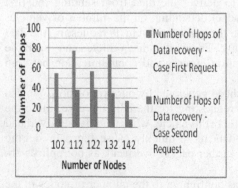
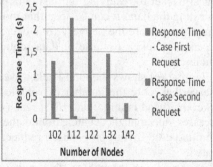

Fig. 4. (a) Numbers of Hops, (b) Response Time / Number of Nodes

Figure 4 shows a comparison study made to demonstrate the benefit gained in terms of number of hops (figure 4 (a)) and latency (figure 4 (b)).

5   Conclusion

In this paper, a new data dissemination and gathering system **RDAP** based on geographical dissemination and data replication mechanism on vehicular sensor networks is proposed. Designed for hybrid VSN architecture, it allows communication between vehicles and between vehicles and road infrastructure. The aim of **RDAP** is to deliver a requested data and make this data accessible for other requesting vehicles. Simulation results of **RDAP** demonstrate the advantage of using the data replication process, the communication between vehicles and the dissemination strategy used to overcome collisions and overhead in the network.

We are currently extending this work by adding new disseminations mode "clusters-based dissemination" and "opportunistic dissemination", data aggregation, meta-data dissemination, and an extensive simulation in order to do a compromise between delivery time and overhead in the network. However, more comprehensive simulation study needs to be conducted to prove the advantage of the protocol. Different comparisons with other VANET or VSN protocols are needed.

References

1. Lee, U., Magistretti, E., Zhou, B., Gerla, M., Bellavista, P., Corradi, A.: Efficient Data Harvesting in Mobile Sensor Platforms. In: IEEE PerSeNS 2006 Workshop, Pisa, Italy (March 2006)
2. Salhi, I., Cherif, M.O., Senouci, S.M.: A New Architecture for Data Collection in Vehicular Networks. 978-1-4244-3435-0/09/$25.00 ©2009 IEEE (2009)
3. Ni, S.Y., Tseng, Y.C., Chen, Y.S., Sheu, J.: The Broadcast storm problem in a mobile ad hoc networks. In: Proc. 5th Annual ACM/IEEE International Conference on Mobile Computing and Networking, Seattle, Washington (August 1999)
4. Kheroua, L., Moussaoui, S., Mansour, L.: An Agent based Rumor Dissemination for Routing in Wireless Sensor Networks. In: ISPS, Algeria (2011)
5. Yang, L., Xu, J., Wu, G., Guo, J.: Road Probing: RSU Assisted Data Collection in Vehicular Networks. IEEE (2009)
6. Hull, B., Bychkovsky, V., Zhang, Y., Chen, K., Goraczko, M., Miu, A., Shih, E., Balakrishnan, H., Madden, S.: CarTel: A Distributed Mobile Sensor Computing System (2006)
7. Lim, K.W., Jung, W.S., Ko, Y.-B.: Multi-Hop Data Dissemination with Replicas in Vehicular Sensor Networks. In: Proceeding Vehicular Technology Conference, VTC Spring 2008, Singapore, May 11-14, pp. 3062–3066. IEEE (2008) ISSN: 1550-2252, ISBN: 978-1-4244-1644-8
8. Mariyasagayam, M., Osafune, T., Lenardi, M.: Enhanced Multi-Hop Vehicular Broadcast (MHVB) for Active Safety Applications. In: Proceedings of the 7th International Conference on ITS Telecommunications, ITST 2007, Sophia-Antipolis, France, pp. 1–6 (June 2007)

9. Seth, A., Darragh, P., Liang, S., Lin, Y., Keshav, S.: An Architecture for Tetherless Communication. In: DTN Workshop (2005)
10. Al Agha, K., Pujolle, G., Vivier, G.: Réseaux de mobiles et réseaux sans fil, Eyrolles (2001)
11. Sun, M.T., Feng, W., Lai, T., Yamada, K., Okada, H., Fujimura, K.: GPS based message broadcast for adaptive inter-vehicle communications. In: Proceedings of the IEEE Vehicular Technology Conference, VTC 2000, Boston, USA, vol. 1, pp. 2685–2692 (September 2000)
12. Little, T.D.C., Agarwal, A.: An Information Propagation Scheme for VANETs. In: Proceedings of the 8th IEEE Conference on Intelligent Transportation Systems, ITSC 2005, Vienna, Austria, pp. 155–160 (September 2005)
13. Benslimane, A.: Optimized Dissemination of Alarm Messages in Vehicular Ad-Hoc Networks (VANET). In: Mammeri, Z., Lorenz, P. (eds.) HSNMC 2004. LNCS, vol. 3079, pp. 655–666. Springer, Heidelberg (2004)
14. Nzouonta, J., Borcea, C.: STEID: A Protocol for Emergency Information Dissemination in Vehicular Networks. Report, Department of Computer Science, New Jersey Institute of Technology (2006)
15. Wu, H., Fujimoto, R., Guensler, R., Hunter, M.: MDDV: a mobility centric data dissemination algorithm for vehicular networks. In: ACM International Workshop on VANETs, Philadelphia, USA (October 2004)
16. Datta, A.: Autonomous Gossiping: A Self-organizing Epidemic Algorithm for Selective Information Dissemination in Wireless Mobile Ad hoc Networks. In: ICDCS 2003 Doctoral Symposium, Providence, Rhode Island USA (May 2003)
17. Bononi, L., Di Felice, M.: A Cross Layered MAC and Clustering Scheme for Efficient Broadcast in VANETs. In: IEEE MASS 2007, Pisa, Italy (October 2007)
18. Bellavista, P., et al.: Standard Integration of Sensing and Opportunistic Diffusion for Urban Monitoring in Vehicular Sensor Networks: the MobEyes Architecture. In: IEEE ISIE 2007 (2007)
19. ns-2 (The Network Simulator), http://www.isi.edu/nsnam/ns
20. Krajzewicz, D., Rossel, C.: Simulation of Urban Mobility (SUMO). German Aerospace Centre (2007), http://sumo.sourceforge.net/index.shtml
21. MOVE (MObility model generator for VEhicular networks): Rapid Generation of Realistic Simulation for VANET (2007),
http://lens1.csie.ncku.edu.tw/MOVE/index.html

An Adaptive Cross-Layer Approach
for Energy-Efficient and QoS-Constrained Multimedia
Transmission over Wireless Channels*

Alfio Lombardo, Carla Panarello, and Giovanni Schembra

Dipartimento di Ingegneria Elettrica, Elettronica e Informatica, University of Catania, Italy
{lombardo,carla.panarello,schembra}@diiei.unict.it

Abstract. The main goal of research and industrial work in wireless telecommunications has been to maximize performance or reduce energy consumption to lengthen the battery life of mobile devices. The challenge in the next future is to make green telecommunications networks, and specifically wireless devices that present the highest energy consumption coefficient per bit transmitted among all the networking devices. However, making a network device green can cause performance deterioration. The target of this paper is to propose a cross-layer approach for the transmission of multiplexed rate-controlled multimedia streams over wireless channels. The proposed approach is adaptive in both the video sources and the wireless transmitter. To this purpose this paper proposes an Energy-efficient ARQ protocol with five possible transmission laws, in order to exploit the correlation of the wireless channel behavior. In addition, in order to compensate transmission bandwidth reduction due to the energy saving policies, a source Rate Controller is introduced. Finally, using an analytical model of the system, the transmission laws are compared, and some guidelines are provided to choose one of them and design its parameters.

Keywords: Wireless communications, Energy-efficiency, Cross-layer approach, ARQ, Video transmission, Performance Evaluation.

1 Introduction

Advances in wireless transmission technology in the last decade have supported an enormous diffusion of portable computers and new generation cellular phones on the one hand, on the other have favored the realization of very complex widespread wireless networks. In this context, mobile access to multimedia applications such as on-demand streaming to mobile devices is one of the most exciting services for next generation networks [1,2].

At the same time, in the last few years power consumption has become very relevant in our life, and there is EU-wide incentive to reduce carbon dioxide emissions by 20 % before year 2020. More in deep, 3 % is expected to come from the ICT sector and

---

* The research leading to these results has received funding from the European Union Seventh Framework Programme (FP7/2007-2013) under grant agreement n. 257740 (Network of Excellence "TREND").

J. Lloret Mauri and J.J.P.C. Rodrigues (Eds.): GreeNets 2012, LNICST 113, pp. 47–59, 2013.

a major role in "greening" telecommunications will be played by wireless networking technologies. For this reason, if up to now the main goal of research and industrial work in telecommunications has been to maximize performance, or reduce energy consumption in mobile devices to lengthen their battery life, the challenge in the next future will be to realize green telecommunications networks, and specifically wireless devices that present the highest energy consumption coefficient per transmitted bit, among all the networking devices.

In this perspective a significant amount of works have been done in recent years to make both wired [3,4,5,6,7,8] and wireless transmissions energy efficient [21,17]. More specifically, in wireless networks the most part of them have been devoted to save energy in low-power battery devices, with the aim of increasing their lifetime [20,18]. Since the launch of 3G access, mobile networks are a major consumer of electricity, and with LTE mobile operators have to prepare for even further increases in power consumption per base station. The energy bill of current deployed wireless networks is already more than significant, surpassing the 20 % of the operating costs for some of them. Thus, means to lower the energy consumption of wireless networks are very valuable. Unfortunately, the power amount necessary for efficient and reliable transmissions makes wireless network devices, like wireless routers and network interfaces, the most critical devices to be optimized. Therefore, greening a wireless network device can cause performance deterioration. It is widely accepted that a good way to improve performance from the network level to the application level is to use a cross-layer approach [25,23,24]. However, it is challenging to maintain perceived Quality of Service (QoS) acceptable when energy saving strategies are implemented.

Energy consumed for efficient wireless transmissions is strongly related to techniques for maintaining reliable communications over noisy channels, such as forward error correction (FEC) and automatic repeat request (ARQ). However, the channel-state unaware behavior makes both FEC and traditional ARQ techniques energy inefficient. For this reason, some channel-adaptive link layer protocol ideas, such as GBN-ARQ and SR-ARQ based on channel probing [28,27], and ARQ based on stochastic learning automaton [22], have been proposed earlier.

Now a challenging task for a successful deployment of mobile video services is to focus at the same time both power consumption at the transmission level and quality of service (QoS) at the application level, with the aim of providing system designers with a tool for achieving a tradeoff between these two above opposite targets.

With this in mind, in this paper we address an energy efficient cross-layer video transmission system over wireless channels consisting of both a channel-adaptive ARQ-based protocol and an adaptive video transmission system. The whole system we address is therefore adaptive in both video source coding and ARQ transmission. More specifically, we propose a new version of the SW-ARQ, in the following referred to as Energy-Efficient ARQ (EE-ARQ), with five possible transmission laws, in order to exploit the correlation of the wireless channel behavior, so minimizing transmission when the channel state is bad. In addition, in order to compensate transmission bandwidth reduction due to the energy saving policies, a Rate Controller is introduced to follow a feedback law to control the encoding rate of the sources. Finally, using an analytical model of the system, the transmission laws are compared, and some guideline is provided to choose one of them and design its parameters.

The paper is structured as follows. Section 2 describes the proposed Green Adaptive Video Wireless Transmission system we consider in the rest of the paper. Section 3 introduces the Markov model of the system and defines the main performance parameters regarding both video encoding quality, queue, ARQ transmission and consumed power. In Section 4 the model is then applied to a case study to evaluate the performance of a real case, and derive some guidelines on choosing the best transmission law and its parameters. Finally, Section 5 concludes the paper.

2 System Description

In this section we will describe the *Green Adaptive Video Wireless Transmission* system we consider in the rest of the paper. It is constituted by a *Video Multiplexer* loaded by V *Adaptive Video Sources* connected to it through high-speed low-delay links. The *Video Multiplexer Queue* is served by a wireless channel with time-variant bit error rate (BER) behavior; channel losses are managed with the Automatic Repeat reQuest (ARQ) protocol. The wireless output link constitutes the system bottleneck. When channel conditions get worse, more retransmissions are needed and the Video Multiplexer queue length increases. In order to avoid congestion, video sources are adaptive, that is their emission bit rate is modified by a *Rate Controller* [9,10] located in the Video Multiplexer, according to the state of the Video Multiplexer Queue, with a mechanism described later in this section.

Adaptive Video Sources we are considering are any video sources that, according to a given feedback, can modify their encoding rate run time in order to change their emission rate [11,12,13,14,15]. Let Ψ be the encoding rate array, containing all the available emission bit rates of the video sources, and Ω the quality array, containing the quality levels associated to the available emission bit rates, expressed in terms of peak signal to noise ratio (PSNR); let G be the number of encoding levels, that is, the cardinality of the sets Ψ and Ω.

Packets coming from video sources are subdivided in *ARQ blocks* of H bits to be managed by the ARQ protocol. These ARQ blocks are buffered in the Video Multiplexer Queue whose dimension, defined as the maximum number of blocks that can be accommodated in the queue and in the server facility, is K. Let C be the transmission rate on the wireless link, expressed in bits per second. Thus the time needed to transmit one ARQ block is $\Delta_{ARQ} = H/C$.

In the considered scenario the most appropriate version of ARQ is the stop-and-wait ARQ (SW-ARQ) because delays introduced by it are not too high, given that link propagation delays are negligible as compared to the ARQ block transmission time; on the other hand it ensures that packets are received at destination in the same order as they were sent by the transmitter.

In this paper we propose a modified version of the SW-ARQ protocol, in order to make it energy efficient. We will refer to this new protocol as EE-ARQ (Energy-Efficient ARQ). The motivation at the base of it is that the quality behavior of the underlying wireless transmission channel is a strongly-correlated stochastic process, that is, the same signal-to-noise ratio (SNR) level is maintained for a period that is very long as compared to the transmission duration of a single ARQ block. For this reason, if a transmission has failed, it is highly likely that an immediately successive attempt will follow the same sort. Starting from this consideration, we propose to use a retransmission policy where the transmission is attempted with a probability depending on the number of previous attempts. In such a way, the sender deduces the state of the channel and transmits more rarely when the channel is considered bad. Of course, the choice of the retransmission policy is expected to have a big impact on the performance in terms of both energy-efficiency and QoS, depending on the channels conditions. For this reason, we consider several retransmission policies and compare them in different scenarios. More specifically, as in the classical SW-ARQ protocol, let ρ be the counter of transmission attempts already done for the same ARQ block ($\rho = 0$ when the block is transmitted for the first time). The counter ρ is incremented by one at each retransmission attempt, and reset to zero when a block is removed from the service facility because successfully transmitted or discarded because the maximum number of retransmissions, $s_{MAX}^{(R)}$, has been reached. According to the new EE-ARQ protocol, in a generic instant when the sender should transmit a block according to the classical SW-ARQ protocol, the transmission is attempted with a probability $\wp^{(Tx)}(\rho)$ depending on the number of previous attempts, ρ. It is defined as:

$$\wp^{(Tx)}(\rho) = \frac{1}{Tx_{law}(\rho)} \tag{1}$$

where $Tx_{law}(\rho)$ is the transmission law associated to the retransmission policy. In this paper we consider and analyze five different transmission laws for the probability to attempt a block transmission. These transmission laws are defined as follows:

- *Exponential*: This retransmission policy is similar to the exponential backoff adopted by IEEE 802.3 CSMA/CD protocol. When this policy is adopted, the transmission law, i.e. the denominator of the probability to attempt a transmission, increases exponentially with the number of previous attempts of retransmission. It is defined as:

$$Tx_{law}(\rho) = \gamma^{\rho}, \text{ with } \gamma \geq 1 \text{ and } \rho \in \{0, \ldots, s_{MAX}^{(R)}\} \tag{2}$$

- *1-Linear*: When this retransmission policy is adopted, the transmission law increases linearly with the number of previous attempts of retransmission. It is defined as:

$$Tx_{law}(\rho) = \begin{cases} 1 & \text{if } \rho = 0 \\ \gamma \cdot \rho, \text{ with } \gamma \geq 1 & \text{if } \rho \in \{1, \ldots, s_{MAX}^{(R)}\} \end{cases} \tag{3}$$

- *Constant*: When this retransmission policy is adopted, the transmission law, and so the probability to attempt a transmission, is constant and does not depend on the number of previous attempts of retransmission. It is defined as:

$$Tx_{law}(\rho) = \begin{cases} 1 & \text{if } \rho = 0 \\ \gamma, \text{ with } \gamma \geq 1 & \text{if } \rho \in \{1, \ldots, s_{MAX}^{(R)}\} \end{cases} \tag{4}$$

- *D-Linear*: When this retransmission policy is adopted the transmission law decrease linearly with the number of previous attempts of retransmission. It is defined as:

$$Tx_{law}(\rho) = \begin{cases} 1 & \text{if } \rho = 0 \\ \gamma \cdot (s_{MAX}^{(R)} - \rho + 1), \text{ with } \gamma \geq 1 & \text{if } \rho \in \{1, \ldots, s_{MAX}^{(R)}\} \end{cases} \tag{5}$$

- *Monomial*: When this retransmission policy is adopted the transmission law increases polynomially with the number of previous attempts of retransmission. More specifically, we consider polynomial functions with only one term. The probability to attempt a transmission is defined as:

$$Tx_{law}(\rho) = \begin{cases} 1 & \text{if } \rho = 0 \\ \rho^{\gamma}, \text{ with } \gamma \geq 1 & \text{if } \rho \in \{1, \ldots, s_{MAX}^{(R)}\} \end{cases} \tag{6}$$

Using these laws allows the sender to deduce the state of the channel to transmit more rarely when the channel is bad. As we will see in Section 4, the choice of the particular law together with the choice of γ have a strong impact on the overall system performance in terms of both application quality and energy consumption.

As already observed so far, the task of the *Rate Controller* is to control the emission bit rate of the video sources with the target of maintaining the queue length as much constant as possible, avoiding situations in which the buffer empties or overflows due to some channel condition variations. To this purpose the Rate Controller periodically monitors the state s_Q of the Video Multiplexer Queue, defined as the number of ARQ blocks which are present in the queue and in the service facility; based on it, the Rate Controller implements a feedback law that determines at each time slot whether sending "rate-increase" or "rate-decrease" feedback messages to the video sources. In order to tune the system reaction time, the Rate Controller decides the number of sources that have to change their rates. More specifically, at each time slot, the Rate Controller first decides the kind of message to send to the video sources according to the state of the queue: when s_Q is less than a given threshold q_L, it sends "rate-increase" messages, while it sends "rate-decrease" messages when s_Q is greater than another threshold, q_H; no messages are sent when $s_Q \in [q_L, q_H]$. Then the Rate Controller decides the number of sources that have to receive the above messages. This number is calculated as $\tilde{v}(s_Q) = \phi \cdot f_{law}(s_Q)$, where $f_{law}(s_Q)$ is the per-source feedback law mask defined as follows:

$$f_{law}(s_Q) = \begin{cases} -\frac{s_Q}{q_L} + 1 & 0 \leq s_Q < q_L \\ 0 & q_L \leq s_Q \leq q_H \\ \frac{s_Q - q_H}{K - q_H} & q_H < s_Q \leq K \end{cases} \tag{7}$$

The function f_{law} is shown in Fig. 1. The coefficient $\phi \in \{1, \cdots, V\}$ allows the Rate Controller to decide the maximum number of sources that can be contacted simultaneously.

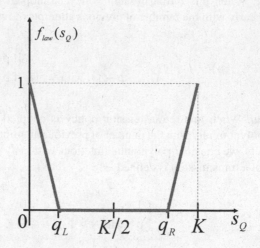

Fig. 1. Feedback law

Since the number $\tilde{v}(s_Q)$ may not be an integer, it is rounded to one of the closest integer values with probabilities proportional to its distance from them. So the final number of sources that have to change their rate is given by:

$$v(s_Q) = \begin{cases} \lfloor \tilde{v}(s_Q) \rfloor & \text{with probability: } 1 - \wp_V(s_Q) \\ \lfloor \tilde{v}(s_Q) \rfloor + 1 & \text{with probability: } \wp_V(s_Q) \\ 0 & \text{otherwise} \end{cases} \qquad (8)$$

where $\wp_V(s_Q) = \tilde{v}(s_Q) - \lfloor \tilde{v}(s_Q) \rfloor$, and $\lfloor x \rfloor$ indicates the maximum integer lower than or equal to x. The $v(s_Q)$ sources to be contacted are randomly chosen among the V sources loading the buffer, starting from the ones encoding at the highest bit rate if $s_Q \in [q_H + 1, K]$, or from the ones encoding at the lowest bit rate, if $s_Q \in [0, q_L - 1]$.

The parameters q_L and q_H can be used to tune the reaction time of the system against the stability of the quality of service perceived at the user level: the higher the distance between q_L and q_R, the less reactive the system, but the more stable the encoding quality.

3   System Model

In this section we describe the Markov model the Green Adaptive Wireless Transmission system described in the previous section, and in the following indicated as Σ. For space problems, we limit to briefly introduce the model, referring the reader to [26] for details. As already said, it is a queueing system loaded by an aggregate of V video adaptive sources, and served by a wireless channel with the energy efficient EE-ARQ mechanism described so far. The model is defined by using the most general Markov-modulated process in the discrete-time domain, the Switched Batch Bernoulli process (SBBP) [16]. The so-called ARQ reaction period, indicated as Δ, and defined as the time needed to transmit an ARQ block and receive the relative ack on the wireless link, is used as the time slot.

Let us define the following processes: 1) the *queue drain process* of this system, $N(p)$, representing the number of ARQ blocks removed from the system in the p-th slot; 2) the emission process of the Adaptive Source aggregate, $W(p)$, representing the number of ARQ blocks sent to the queue from the source aggregate during the p-th slot. A complete description of the system Σ at the p-th slot requires a two-dimensional Markov chain, whose state in the generic p-th slot is defined as $\underline{S}^{(\Sigma)}(p) = \left(\underline{S}^{(W)}(p), \underline{S}^{(S)}(p) \right)$, where:

- $\underline{S}^{(W)}(p)$ is the state of the underlying Markov chain of the adaptive source aggregate emission process $W(p)$. It is a vector of G elements; the g-th element, for $g \in \{1, ..., G\}$, represents the number of sources using the g-th encoding level for the frame to be encoded in the p-th slot;
- $\underline{S}^{(S)}(p)$ is the state of the Markov chain of the queueing system process; it is a two-dimensional Markov chain defined as $\underline{S}^{(S)}(p) = \left(S^{(Q)}(p), \underline{S}^{(N)}(p) \right)$ where:
  - $S^{(Q)}(p) \in \{0, ..., K\}$ is the queue state, i.e. the number of ARQ blocks in the queue and in the server facility at the p-th slot;
  - $\underline{S}^{(N)}(p)$ is the state of the Markov chain characterizing the queue drain process $N(p)$; it is defined as $\underline{S}^{(N)}(p) = \left(S^{(R)}(p), S^{(C)}(p) \right)$, where $S^{(R)}(p)$ and $S^{(C)}(p)$ are the retransmission state and the channel state, respectively.

Now, by solving the system Markov chain as shown in [26], we can derive the following main QoS parameters:

- $\overline{psnr}$, defined as the mean peak signal-to-noise ratio characterizing the encoding process of the video sources;
- $\wp_{Loss_{ARQ}}$, defined as the loss probability due to the fact that some ARQ blocks have been retransmitted for a number of times greater than the maximum limit $s_{MAX}^{(R)}$.

In order to evaluate the energy saving amount introduced by the proposed protocol, from the analytical model we derive the total power consumption as follows:

$$\overline{P} = \overline{P}_{Tx_{SUCCESS}} + \overline{P}_{Tx_{FAILURE}} + \overline{P}_{IDLE} \qquad (9)$$

where $\overline{P}_{Tx_{SUCCESS}} = P_{Tx} \cdot \wp_{Tx_{SUCCESS}}$, $\overline{P}_{Tx_{FAILURE}} = P_{Tx} \cdot \wp_{Tx_{FAILURE}}$, and $\overline{P}_{IDLE} = P_{IDLE} \cdot \wp_{IDLE}$ represent the power consumed during a successful transmission, a failed transmission and an ARQ transmitter IDLE state (corresponding to a state when the transmitter is idle because the queue is empty, or the EE-ARQ algorithm imposes the transmitter to not transmit in order to save power). The terms P_{Tx} and P_{IDLE} are input parameters, representing the power consumed in one slot to transmit an ARQ block or to be in the IDLE state, respectively. The terms $\wp_{Tx_{SUCCESS}}$, $\wp_{Tx_{FAILURE}}$ and $\wp_{IDLE}$ are the probabilities of a successful transmission, a failed transmission and a transmitter IDLE state, respectively.

4   Numerical Results

In this section we numerically evaluate the cross-layer approach proposed for the Green Adaptive Video Wireless Transmission system. The evaluation will be carried out in terms of both quality of service and power saving, with the purpose of deducing some design guidelines on the choice of the best EE-ARQ protocol transmission law among the ones defined so far, according to the given requirements specified in terms of QoS and power saving.

In the following we consider a video sequence in CIF format (352 x 288 pixels), related to a documentary captured from the BBC International Television, and encoded using the vcodec mpeg2video with the ffmpeg encoder. We have applied $G = 5$ different encoding levels ($\Psi = \{80, 120, 160, 200, 240\}$kbit/s). The correspondent PSNR values are: $\Omega = \{39.5, 44.0, 46.0, 47.5, 49.0\}$ dB. In both the analysis we have set a number of sources of $V = 10$ and a buffer size of $K = 25$ ARQ blocks. Each ARQ block is constituted by $H = 512$ bits, the maximum number of retransmissions is $s_{MAX}^{(R)} = 7$. For space problems, we limited our analysis using a Rate Controller with a V-shaped feedback mask, i.e. $q_L = q_R = K/2$, with a parameter $\phi = 1/V$ in such a way that only one source at time is requested to change its encoding rate.

As far as the wireless transmission side is concerned, we used a channel bitrate C of 5Mb/s; therefore the slot duration is $\Delta_{ARQ} = H/C = 0.1$ms. According to [19], we assumed that the wireless interface consumes a power of $\mathcal{P}_{Tx} = 1350$ mW during transmission, and $\mathcal{P}_{IDLE} = 66$ mW when it is idle. Although the analytical model is able to capture both first- and second-order statistics of the channel behavior, here we present an analysis for a constant BER, equal to $1 \cdot 10^{-3}$; in this way our results are independent on the channel time correlation.

First we evaluate QoS performance at both the queue level, in terms of mean queue length and loss probability, and the application level, in terms of encoding PSNR. Figs. 2 and 3 show the mean queue length and the overall loss probability against the transmission law parameter γ for all the five transmission laws defined in Section 2. The overall loss probability has been calculated by summing the contribution of the loss probability due to buffer overflow and the probability of losses caused by the fact that the number of retransmissions of some ARQ block has exceeded the maximum allowed value $s_{MAX}^{(R)}$. Of course, the two curves relating to the Exponential and the Constant laws coincide with the classical ARQ protocols for $\gamma = 1$. As expected, we can observe that all the proposed laws, for any value of the parameter γ, present worse performance than the classical ARQ. This is due to the fact that ARQ is the most aggressive, since it tries transmission at each slot, independently of the result of the previous transmissions. However we can observe that the mean queue length achieved with the classical ARQ is less than the intermediate value $K/2$. This means that feedback provided by the Rate Controller to the video sources does not work as desired because all the sources encode to their maximum rate, but some channel capacity is wasted. Instead, the I-Linear, Exponential and Monomial laws with $\gamma \in [1, 2]$ achieve a mean queue length very close to $K/2$. On the contrary, the D-Linear law is too conservative in transmitting on the wireless channel, and therefore is not able to adequately serve the queue. The same problem is present, as expected, when the Exponential or the Monomial laws are used with $\gamma > 2.5$.

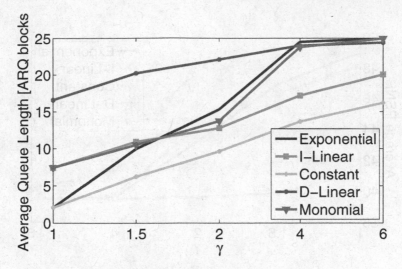

Fig. 2. Average Queue Length

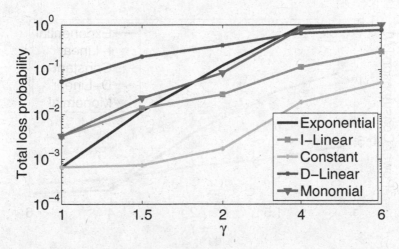

Fig. 3. Loss probability

User level performance is represented by the PSNR parameter shown in Fig. 4 calculated, as for the previous parameters, against γ and for each of the transmission law. According to the cross-layer approach adopted by the proposed system, higher PSNR values are obtained when the Rate Controller allows sources to encode with a higher rate, and this occurs when the mean queue length is lower. This is the reason why the PSNR graphics are specular in respect to the ones in Fig. 2. From the above figures we can note that the higher the value of γ the worse the performance.

However, using the proposed transmission laws and increasing the γ parameter provide power saving. To quantify the gain in power saving, Fig. 5 shows the total power consumed by the wireless transmitter for all the considered laws. From this figure we can observe a power saving gain in respect to the classical ARQ, corresponding to

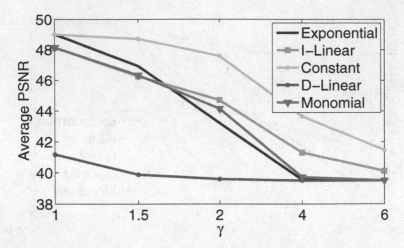

Fig. 4. Average PSNR

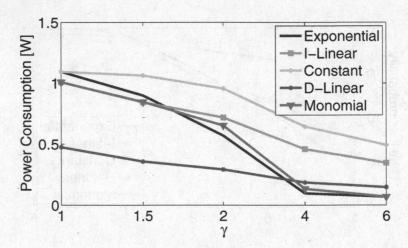

Fig. 5. Power consumption

the point of the Constant and the Exponential laws calculated for $\gamma = 1$, and this gain increases with the γ parameter. More specifically, the most power efficient law is the D-Linear one, but it presents too low performance in terms of average delay, loss probability and PSNR, as discussed so far. Instead, for γ greater than or equal to 2 the Exponential and the Monomial laws present high efficiency if compared with the classical ARQ. No appreciable power gain is achieved by the Constant law.

Finally, in order to deduce some design guidelines on both the choice of the best law and the best γ parameter, in Figs. 6 and 7 we combine results shown in Figs. 5, 3 and 4 to show the consumed power vs. the achieved loss probability and PSNR, respectively.

The above curves can be used as follows. Let us assume a two state channel, with a bad state characterized by a BER of 10^{-3}. If for example we require that the overall loss

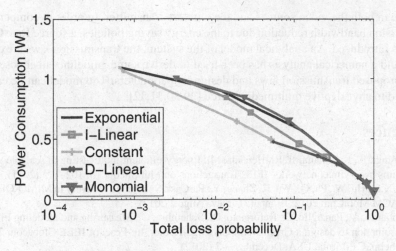

Fig. 6. Power consumption vs. loss probability

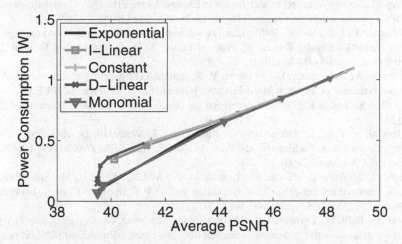

Fig. 7. Power consumption vs. PSNR

probability during this state is not greater than $5 \cdot 10^{-2}$, we can save 10% of the power if we use the Monomial law instead of the classical ARQ. If even greater loss probabilities can be tolerated because recovered in intervals when the channel will be good, the Exponential law allows power saving greater than 50%. This is also paid by decreasing the encoding PSNR, as shown in Fig. 4. So, according to two maximum thresholds on loss probability and PSNR, we can use these figures to derive the minimum power needed to obtain the required performance, and decide the transmission law to be used.

5   Conclusions

In this paper we have proposed a cross-layer approach for the transmission of multiplexed rate-controlled multimedia streams over wireless channels. The proposed approach is adaptive in both the video sources and the wireless transmitter. In order to compensate transmission bandwidth reduction due to the energy saving policies, a source Rate Controller is introduced. An analytical model of the system, the transmission laws are compared, and a numerical analysis has been used to derive some guidelines to choose one of the proposed transmission laws and design its parameters. The model can be easily extended to any adaptive multimedia source [29,30,31,32].

References

1. Sharangi, S., Krishnamurti, R., Hefeeda, M.: Energy-efficient multicasting of scalable video streams over wimax networks. IEEE Transactions on Multimedia 13, 102–115 (2011)
2. Liu, X.L., Hu, W., Pu, Q., Wu, F., Zhang, Y.: ParCast: Soft Video Delivery in MIMO-OFDM. In: ACM MobiCom 2012, Istanbul, Turkey (August 2012)
3. Lombardo, A., Panarello, C., Reforgiato, D., Schembra, G.: Measuring and modeling Energy Consumption to design a Green NetFPGA Giga-Router. In: Proc. of IEEE Globecom 2012, Anaheim, California, USA, December 3-7 (2012)
4. Bolla, R., Bruschi, R., Davoli, F., Cucchietti, F.: Energy Efficiency in the Future Internet: A Survey of Existing Approaches and Trends in Energy-Aware Fixed Netweork Infrastuctures. IEEE Communications Surveys & Tutorials 13(2), 223–244 (2011)
5. Lombardo, A., Panarello, C., Reforgiato, D., Schembra, G.: Power control and management in the NetFPGA Gigabit Router. In: Proc. of Future Network and Mobile Summit 2012, Berlin, Germany, July 04-06 (2012)
6. Lombardo, A., Reforgiato, D., Riccobene, V., Schembra, G.: Modeling Temperature and Dissipation Behavior of an Open Multi-FrequencyGreen Router. In: Proc. of IEEE GreenCom 2012, The Second IEEE Online Conference on Green Communications, September 25-28 (2012)
7. Nedevschi, S., Popa, L., Iannaccone, G., Ratnasamy, S., Wetherall, D.: Reducing Network Energy Consumption via Sleeping and Rate-Adaptation. In: USENIX/ACM NSDI 2008, San Francisco, USA (April 2008)
8. Panarello, C., Ajmone Marsan, M., Lombardo, A., Mellia, M., Meo, M., Schembra, G.: On the Intertwining between Capacity Scaling and TCP Congestion Control. In: Proc. of e-Energy 2012, Madrid, Spain, May 9-11 (2012)
9. Favalli, L., Folli, M., Lombardo, A., Reforgiato, D., Schembra, G.: Design of a service platform for delay-sensitive video streaming applications based on multicast p2p and scalable MDC encoding. Computer Communications 35(18), 2254–2263 (2012)
10. Lombardo, A., Reforgiato, D., Schembra, G.: P2P and MPEG FGS Encoding: A Good Recipe for Multipoint Video Transmission on the Internet. International Journal of Digital Multimedia Broadcasting 2009, Article ID 453471, 21 pages (2009)
11. Lombardo, A., Schembra, G.: Performance evaluation of an Adaptive-Rate MPEG encoder matching IntServ Traffic Constraints. IEEE Transactions on Networking 11(1), 47–65 (2003)
12. Jurca, D., Chakareski, J., Wagner, J.P., Frossard, P.: Enabling adaptive video streaming in P2P systems. IEEE Communications Magazine 45(6), 108–114 (2007)
13. Duffield, N.G., Ramakrishnan, K.K., Reibman, A.R.: SAVE: an algorithm for smoothed adaptive video over explicit rate networks. In: Proc. of IEEE INFOCOM 1998, March 29-April 2 (1998)
14. Vandalore, B., Feng, W.C., Jain, R., Fahmy, S.: A Survey of Application Layer Techniques for Adaptive Streaming of Multimedia. Real-Time Imaging 7(3), 221–235 (2001)
15. Schembra, G.: A Resource Management Strategy for Multimedia Adaptive-Rate Traffic in a Wireless Network with TDMA Access. IEEE Transactions on Wireless Communications 4(1), 65–78 (2005)

16. La Corte, A., Lombardo, A., Schembra, G.: An Analytical Paradigm to Calculate Multiplexer Performance in an ATM Multimedia Environment. Computer Networks and ISDN Systems 29(16) (December 1997)
17. Son, K., Krishnamachari, B.: SpeedBalance: Speed-Scaling-Aware Optimal Load Balancing for Green Cellular Networks. In: IEEE Infocom 2012 (2012)
18. Chen, S., Shroff, N.B., Sinha, P.: A Simple Asymptotically Optimal Energy Allocation and Routing Scheme in Rechargeable Sensor Networks. In: IEEE Infocom 2012 (2012)
19. Feeney, L.M., Nilsson, M.: Investigating the energy consumption of a wireless network interface in an ad hoc networking environment. In: IEEE Infocom, pp. 1548–1557 (2001)
20. Guo, C., Prasad, R.V., Pawelczak, P., Hekmat, R.: Designing energy efficient automatic repeat request protocol in wireless sensor networks. In: Proceedings of the 4th ACM Workshop on Challenged Networks, CHANTS 2009, pp. 35–42. ACM, New York (2009)
21. Jones, C.E., Sivalingam, K.M., Agrawal, P., Chen, J.-C.: A survey of energy efficient network protocols for wireless networks. Wireless Networks 7, 343–358 (2001)
22. Kumar, K.S., Chandramouli, R., Subbalakshmi, K.P.: On stochastic learning in predictive wireless arq. Wirel. Commun. Mob. Comput. 8, 871–883 (2008)
23. Galluccio, L., Schembra, G., Morabito, G.: Transmission of Adaptive MPEG Video over Time-Varying Wireless Channels: Modeling and Performance Evaluation. IEEE Transactions on Wireless Communications 4(1), 2777–2788 (2005)
24. Galluccio, L., Licandro, F., Morabito, G., Schembra, S.: An analytical framework for the design of intelligent algorithms for adaptive-rate MPEG video encoding in next generation time-varying wireless networks. IEEE Journal on Selected Areas in Communications, Special Issue on Intelligent Services and Applications in Next Generation Networks 23(2), 369–384 (2005)
25. Xu, J., Shen, X., Mark, J., Cai, J.: Adaptive transmission of multi-layered video over wireless fading channels. IEEE Transactions on Wireless Communications 6, 2305–2314 (2007)
26. Lombardo, A., Panarello, C., Reforgiato, D., Schembra, G.: Modeling a cross-layer green video transmission system. TR5.11, www.diit.unict.it/arti/TR/TR5_11.pdf
27. Zorzi, M., Rao, R.R.: Energy constrained error control for wireless channels. IEEE Personal Communications 4, 27–33 (1997)
28. Zorzi, M., Rao, R.R.: Error control and energy consumption in communications for nomadic computing. IEEE Transactions on Computers 46, 279–289 (1997)
29. Colonnese, S., Panci, G., Rinauro, S., Scarano, G.: Markov model OF H.264 video sources performing bit-rate switching. In: Proc. of ICIP 2008, San Diego, CA, USA, October 12-15 (2008)
30. Mahapakulchai, S., Hasajitto, S.: Adaptive MAP source-controlled channel decoding for MPEG-4 imagery wireless transmission systems. In: Proc. of ISCIT 2009, Incheon, Korea, September 28-30 (2009)
31. Lombardo, A., Morabito, G., Schembra, G.: A Discrete-Time Paradigm to Evaluate Skew Performance in a Multimedia ATM Multiplexer. IEEE/ACM Transactions on Networking 7(1) (February 1999)
32. Beritelli, F., Lombardo, A., Palazzo, S., Schembra, G.: Performance Analysis of an ATM Multiplexer Loaded with VBR Traffic Generated by Multimode Speech Coders. IEEE Journal on Selected Areas in Communications 17(1) (January 1999)

Evaluation of Voltage Stabilization
on a SmartGrid Simulation System
for Introduction of EV

Keiko Karaishi and Masato Oguchi

Ochanomizu University,
2-1-1 Ohtsuka, Bunkyo-ku, Tokyo 112-8610, Japan
keiko@ogl.is.ocha.ac.jp, oguchi@computer.org

Abstract. Recently, attention has been focused on whether the Smart-Grid could work efficiently in an energy network. The subject of our study is the electric vehicle (EV), which has been proposed as a potential chargeable/dischargeable part of the power grid infrastructure. As energy is transferred between an EV and the power grid, it is possible to regulate energy on the entire grid via charging and discharging the EV battery. In the future, it may also be possible to stabilize energy within the system, using information technology control embedded in the network of the SmartGrid. Compared with a case in which energy storage is fixed, more complex control is needed when EV technology is used. This study evaluates these circumstances using a simulated system.

Keywords: SmartGrid, EV, V2G, energy network, simulation system.

1 Introduction

Recently, the scarcity of natural resources and rapid increases in energy demands have been raised as worldwide problems; thus, it has become necessary to promote renewable energy generation as a means of energy conservation. However, controlling output power for renewable energy generation is difficult because energy output is subject to violent fluctuations. To address this issue, attention has been focused on the potential for SmartGrid to work efficiently in energy networks.

The electric vehicle (EV) is closely related to the SmartGrid. An EV has a high-capacity battery, and it is not only used as a vehicle but is also treated as a power resource that can charge and discharge energy as needed. This energy exchange is referred to as 'Vehicle-to-Grid' (V2G).

However, V2G power grids are different from traditional power grids that deliver electricity from power plants to users in a single direction. Power resources in V2G power grids are widely distributed within a given area, and electric transmission is bidirectional. In this case, meticulous control regulation to stabilize power flow is necessary, i.e., it is necessary to monitor the electric potential of each point on the grid, to exchange information through the network and to control the distribution of power sources.

J. Lloret Mauri and J.J.P.C. Rodrigues (Eds.): GreeNets 2012, LNICST 113, pp. 60–71, 2013.

In this study, simulation is used as a method to evaluate power control when EVs are connected to the SmartGrid as a power source. First, a power grid simulation environment was constructed, and the impact of EVs connected to the power grid in this simulated environment was evaluated. Specifically, we connected many EVs to the power grid environment, discharged the batteries and monitored the voltage fluctuations at each point.

The remainder of this paper is organized as follows. Section 2 introduces an outline of the SmartGrid and EV. Section 3 summarizes this study. Section 4 describes a model of the distribution network and introduces the implementation of EVs and a solar power plant in an experimental simulation system. Section 5 introduces the results of the simulation connecting EVs as a power source to a power grid. Section 6 presents a conclusion and future directions for this research.

2   Background

2.1   The SmartGrid

There is no clear definition of the 'SmartGrid'. In a broad sense, this term refers to the electric power system that can coordinate and direct the network of electric power energy. Features of this system include the ability to integrate a large amount of renewable energy, to transmit electricity in both directions at the power grids and to manage information as well as energy.

Figure 1 shows the schematic view of a SmartGrid. Figure 1 is a diagram constructed in reference to official documents from the Ministry of Economy, Trade and Industry [1]. Electric power flow (green line) and information control (blue line) are both represented in Figure 1. The SmartGrid includes a large wind power plant, a large solar power plant and solar panels on each home and building, so that electric power can be transmitted bidirectionally. This feature allows the power grids to accept abundant electric power. However, there is a concern that power in the grids will become erratic. Thus, control using IT, an important feature of the SmartGrid, is needed. The control center connects the power grids and monitors the electric power status of every point on the grids through the network. The control center enables electric power stabilization so that power generation is promoted under conditions of energy scarcity, and electric power is stored in the storage facilities under conditions of energy overabundance. As explained above, the SmartGrid is technology that stabilizes the complicated flow of electric power using IT control.

2.2   Relationship between EVs and the SmartGrid

Next, we focus on the utilization of EV power in the SmartGrid. The EV is a vehicle that uses an electric motor instead of an internal combustion engine. In this research, we examine the EV as a source of energy supply and demand.

Recently, the EV has been proposed for use as not only a vehicle but also as a power resource that could charge and discharge energy as needed. This idea has been disseminated in SmartGrid research studies and referenced by the

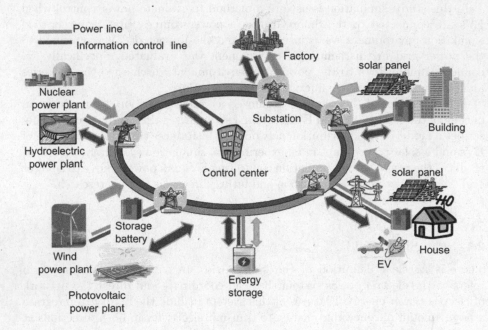

Fig. 1. SmartGrid

term 'V2G'. As EV technology has spread, a huge number of batteries have been distributed in a variety of locations. It is possible to adjust the energy within the entire grid so that the EV batteries discharge in case of energy deficiency on the power grids and electric power is stored in EV batteries in case of an excess of energy on the power grids.

As described above, the use of IT energy stabilization control is indispensable to this system. However, it should be noted that electric power on the grids is subject to violent fluctuations because EVs move freely within the grid. In contrast to a case in which a fixed storage battery is connected to the grid, there are complicated power control issues when using EVs as a power source because EV batteries are worn out by repeated charging and discharging cycles excessively. In this paper, the effect of a solar power plant and EVs on power grids is examined via simulations in which the power output of the solar power plant and the number of EVs discharging at a given time are varied.

3   Research Outline

The purpose of this research is to evaluate the efficient interaction of electric energy between EV batteries and the power grid using simulation.

Based on our research plan, a simulation is constructed that includes a large power grid connected to a power plant and EVs, and the operation of a system for assessment is then verified. Another system is added to manage data communications that adjust the electric power on a grid. Finally, a complex simulation system of the SmartGrid is constructed for final evaluation.

In this paper, we evaluate whether it is possible to perform voltage control through the SmartGrid as well as how much voltage control is appropriate by instructing the EVs to discharge based on the information from a monitor point, assuming that the control function for electric power adjustment operated correctly based on data communications. We set up a power flow simulation that considered output fluctuations from the solar power plant and the number of EVs connected to the home system as a function of time.

4   Experimental Description

4.1   Experimental Environment

The constructed experimental environment was based on a simulation platform by Open Distribution System Simulator (OpenDSS) [2] and a power grid model '8500-Node Test Feeder' provided by IEEE PES (Power & Energy Society) [3]. This power grid model has 8500 nodes and is approximately 10-15 km square. The grid computes power flow based on the specified load. In this model, a voltage source (115 kV, 3000 MVA) with a three-phase electrical power system and the substations to transform from 115 kV to 120/240 V via 7.2 kV are connected to the power grid. The power transmission method of each end node (120/240 V) is a split-phase electrical distribution system, and the load of each end point is 0.005-93.73 kW. The entire grid has a 10773 kW load, i.e., a load of approximately 2000 households.

4.2   Experimental Outline

A solar power plant (2400 kW) at one point in a 7.2 kV area was connected to the power grid model introduced in Section 4.1.

Every end point (2354) in a 120/240 V area has one household, and 20% of the total number of households have a single EV attached. When the electric power on a grid fluctuates abnormally, charging and discharging the EV battery connected to each household stabilizes electric power within the entire grid. Figure 3 shows the model described above.

In this experiment, we further evaluated a situation in which the output of the solar power plant decreased rapidly due to worsening weather. Figure 4 shows the power output of the solar power plant. This output curve was created by reference to data collected by the National Institute of Advanced Industrial Science and Technology (AIST) [4]. We assumed that the output power of the solar power plant drops to 0% during worsening weather. It is assumed that voltage fluctuations occur on the grid when the output from the solar power plant is reduced. Consequently, each EV battery is discharged to compensate for variations in solar power plant output, and electric power within the entire grid is stabilized.

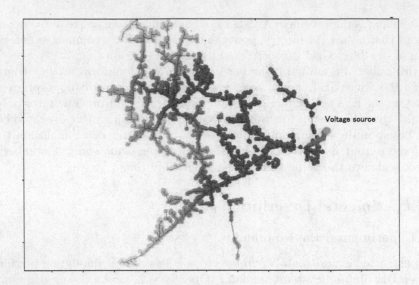

Fig. 2. 8500-Node Test Feeder

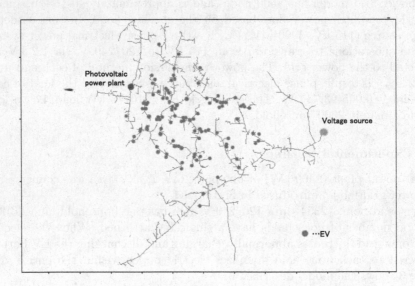

Fig. 3. Experimental system

5   Experimental Result

The monitor points were observed to verify the voltage fluctuations present in the entire power grid resulting from the power output fluctuations at the solar power plant and discharge of EV batteries. The extent of voltage differences at each monitor point on the power grid was surveyed in cases of rainy and fine weather. We assumed that the voltage was within an adequate range if the

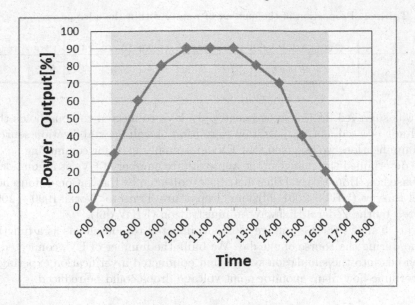

Fig. 4. Output of the solar power plant

voltage difference at each monitor point was -5 V or more with reference to each voltage in the case of fine weather. This range was determined based on the Regulations for Enforcement of the Telecommunications Business Law.

5.1   Voltage Differences Caused by Weather Changes

In this section, the monitor points at 1177 substations transforming electric power from 7.2 kV to 120/240 V were observed to verify voltage fluctuations present in the entire power grid resulting from the power output fluctuations at the solar power plant caused by changes in the weather. Figure 4 shows that each power output difference caused by changes in the weather occurs between 7:00 and 16:00. The simulation system then calculated the voltage difference at each point caused by changes in the weather over time.

Table 1 shows the proportion of the number of points where the voltage differences are identified within the adequate range. The voltage at each monitor point dropped to a lower value because the output power of the solar power plant decreased to 0% in the worsening weather. Between 8:00 and 15:00, the voltage at some points dipped below the adequate range. Therefore, EV discharge is necessary for electric power stabilization of the entire grid between 8:00 and 15:00.

5.2   Voltage Stabilization via EV Discharge

In this section, we performed a verification experiment for the reduction of dropped voltage on the entire grid caused by changes in the weather. Prior to this experiment, the change in the number of available EVs as a function of

Table 1. Proportion of the number of points within the adequate range

Time	7:00	8:00	9:00	10:00	11:00	12:00	13:00	14:00	15:00	16:00
points within normal limits[%]	100.0	82.9	63.4	57.4	57.4	57.4	57.4	68.3	96.8	100.0

time was surveyed. In this experiment, only EVs connected to households that would not be used as transportation were used as voltage stabilization sources. For simplification, we assumed that EVs are mainly used for commuting.

We determined the change in the approximate number of EVs as a function of time based on 'Home arrival time distribute' collected by the National Household Travel Survey (NHTS 2001 [5]) and 'Departure Time to Work: 1990 - 2000' collected by the Federal Highway Administration (FHWA[6]).

Figure 5 shows the percentage of EVs connected to households as a function of time during the course of one day. We built the number of EVs connected to households into the simulation system and conducted a verification experiment to determine how many monitor point voltage drops could be reduced.

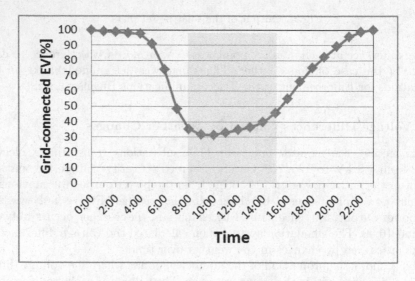

Fig. 5. Number of EVs connected to households over time

In this experiment, the battery capacity of each EV is 25 kWh, and each battery is fully charged. The output power of each EV is 5 kW, and all available EVs are discharged. Figure 6 through Figure 13 show experimental results. Each graph shows 1177 monitor points, for which voltage is observed is plotted on the abscissa and the voltage difference [V] is plotted on the ordinate axis. The range, colored in orange, shows the adequate range within which the voltage difference at each monitor point is -5 V or more with reference to each voltage in the case of fine weather. Each blue point represents the value of decreased voltage in the worsening weather, as described in Section 5.1, and each yellow point represents the voltage value with EV discharge during the same worsening weather. We can see that the voltage increases at every point. However, in these graphs, the voltage at some specific points has risen significantly; these points are nearest the point where the discharging EV is connected, and they are strongly influenced by EV discharge.

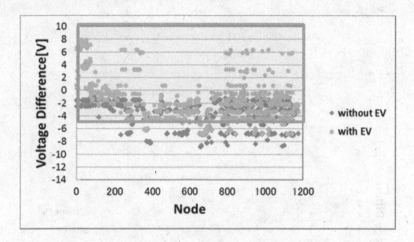

Fig. 6. Voltage difference (8:00)

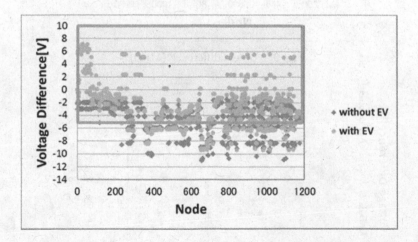

Fig. 7. Voltage difference (9:00)

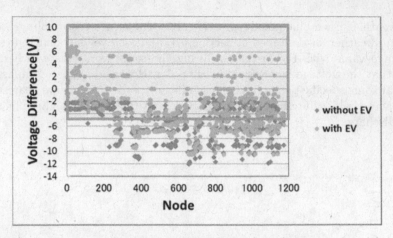

Fig. 8. Voltage difference (10:00)

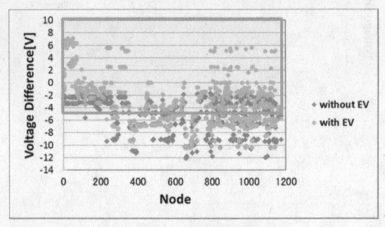

Fig. 9. Voltage difference (11:00)

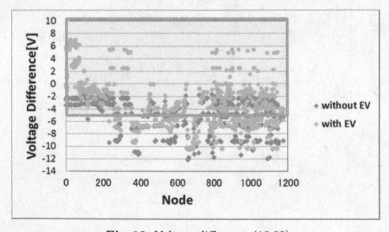

Fig. 10. Voltage difference (12:00)

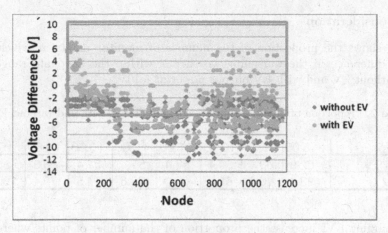

Fig. 11. Voltage difference (13:00)

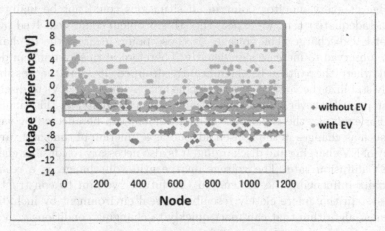

Fig. 12. Voltage difference (14:00)

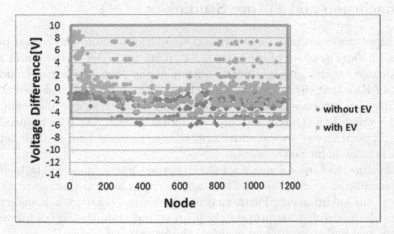

Fig. 13. Voltage difference (15:00)

5.3 Considerations

Table 2 shows the proportion of the number of monitor points at which the voltage difference in the worsening weather is within the adequate range for cases without EV and with EV output power at 5 kW.

Table 2. Proportion of points within the adequate range with and without EV

Time	8:00	9:00	10:00	11:00	12:00	13:00	14:00	15:00
without EV	82.9	63.4	57.4	57.4	57.4	57.4	68.3	96.8
with EV	93.7	70.2	61.9	62.0	63.6	64.5	79.4	100.0

Discharging EVs increase the proportion of the number of points where the voltage difference is within the adequate range. In this experiment, although the voltage at every monitor point in all situations could not be maintained within the adequate range, we expect that this problem could be solved by fine control of EV discharge. The voltages at those points nearest the discharging EVs were observed to increase significantly. Therefore, if this system can detect the point where the voltage has significantly dropped, it would be possible to effectively stabilize the voltage over the whole area by directing EVs to discharge near that point.However, not all conditions were considered in this simulated system. For example, the experimental environment can be affected by various factors, such as changes in the household load as a function of time and variable frequency of EV charging and discharging. It is also necessary to consider changes in the EV diffusion rate. The voltage on the grid will change as a result of these factors influencing the system. In the future, we aim to construct and verify a system that more closely resembles a real environment by including a management algorithm that can react quickly to changing conditions.

6   Conclusion and Future Studies

In this paper, we constructed a SmartGrid simulation system with a solar power plant and EVs. The effect of the solar power plant and EVs on the power grids was evaluated by changing the power output of the solar power plant and the number of EVs that discharged as a function of time. The efficient interaction of electric energy between the EV batteries and power grid was also examined using the simulation. Our results indicated that discharging EVs reduced the voltage drops observed on the entire grid that were caused by weather-related changes in solar plant power output.

In the future, factors to account for electric power fluctuations will be included in this simulation system to construct and verify a system that more closely models a real environment. Furthermore, we aim to construct a management center in the network to appropriately process and stabilize electric power on the entire grid and to verify and evaluate the SmartGrid system.

Acknowledgments. The authors wish to thank Mr. Onur Altintas at the Toyota InfoTechnology Center and Dr. Sekyung Han at the Institute of Industrial Science, the University of Tokyo, for conscientious advice and help with this work.

References

1. Ministry of Economy, Trade and Industry, http://www.meti.go.jp/
2. OpenDSS, http://sourceforge.net/projects/electricdss/
3. IEEE PES, http://www.ieee-pes.org/
4. Agency of Industrial Science and Technology Research Center for Photovoltaic Technologies, http://unit.aist.go.jp/rcpvt/ci/index.html
5. National Household Travel Survey, http://nhts.ornl.gov/
6. Federal Highway Administration, http://www.fhwa.dot.gov/

Capacity Planning for Enterprise Green Communications

Sami J. Habib and Paulvanna N. Marimuthu

Kuwait University
Computer Engineering Department
P.O. Box 5969 Safat 13060 Kuwait
sami.habib@ku.edu.kw

Abstract. Nowadays, the volume of data transferred in an enterprise information network has raised inexorably high, thereby consuming more power and releasing more carbon-di-oxide into the atmosphere. Typical enterprise networks with fiber-optic medium for transferring data at the backbone are forced to limit the increase in backbone traffic to offer a speedy, energy efficient and environment friendly communications. We have proposed a capacity planning scheme based on molecular assembly (MA) to convert a single clustered network into a multi-clustered network, thereby reducing the backbone traffic and managing CO_2 emission. The capacity planning scheme starts by discovering the distance forces existing among the nodes; moreover, it integrates the highly associated nodes together into various clusters. The repeated discovery process and the optimized assembly process form a set of optimized clusters with reduced backbone traffic, thereby reducing CO_2 emissions. Our experimental results within MA for a non-clustered enterprise network of 60 nodes, quantifying backbone traffic and CO_2 emission with oil fuel as the source of electricity generation shows that the proposed MA algorithm manages to reduce the backbone traffic by 42%, and thereby reducing the amount of CO_2 emission by 2.5 tons in a year of operation.

Keywords: carbon footprint, cluster, optimization, molecular assembly, optical-fiber.

1   Introduction

Presently, the Earth retains more warmth from the Sun than it radiates back. The presence of green house gases such as methane, carbon-di-oxide, and nitrous oxide in the atmosphere slow down this radiation, thereby increasing Earth's surface temperature. The industrial revolution increases green house gases emission, whereby the power generations depend on fossil fuels. Moreover, the information and communication industries heavily depend on energy resources, thereby indirectly contributing to global warming.

The enterprise information networks supporting a variety of applications are primarily consists of two levels: backbone and local area network. Most of the enterprise networks deploy optical fiber connectivity at the backbone to manage the heavy traffic flow. The commercially available multi-mode fiber optic cables support

J. Lloret Mauri and J.J.P.C. Rodrigues (Eds.): GreeNets 2012, LNICST 113, pp. 72–80, 2013.

1/2/4 Gbps fiber channels [1]. The ratio of the volume of backbone traffic to the engineered capacity of the channel influences the performance of the network as well as the release of green house gases into the atmosphere, thereby creating a necessity to focus on various strategies to reduce resource utilization and energy consumption. The enterprises utilize wireless networking through wireless fidelity, known as Wi-Fi for local communication confined to shorter distance and low-bandwidth. Most of the Wi-Fi systems transmit data at the rate of 1 to 11 Mbps in the unlicensed 2.4 GHz ISM band, covering up to 100 meter range [2]. However the range varies as a function of transmit power and environment.

In this paper, we present a capacity planning tool based on molecular assembly (MA) to meet the green communication requirements. According to [3][4], some features of molecular assembly can be exploited to reassemble the system by examining the attraction forces holding the components within the system. Our simulation results for the given medium sized, enterprise network of 60 nodes synthesized through MA show an improvement in performance by reducing the backbone traffic up to 42% and also by reducing CO_2 emission by 53%.

The rest of the paper is organized into six sections, where section 2 surveys the related work. Section 3 details the capacity planning through MA. Section 4 describes problem formulation and Section 5 describes the power estimation. Section 6 presents a detailed analysis of the computational results and Section 7 concludes the paper.

2   Related Work

Researchers have made various feasibility studies on capacity planning of enterprise networks through optimizing the usage of resources. Ragunath and Ramakrishnan [5] suggested a set of techniques to build an adaptively provisioned virtual private network (VPN) to deal with dynamic customer traffic. Gmach et al. [6] proposed and evaluated the aspects of a capacity management process for automating the efficient use of resource pools of a server to host large numbers of services. They applied a trace based measurement and they claimed 35% reduction in the processor usage with the proposed capacity management process.

Few researchers analyzed the importance of optical routing at the backbone to manage the heavy traffic [7] and few others introduced various strategies to minimize the backbone traffic, thereby saving the energy consumption and reducing environmental carbon footprint [8][9].

The self-organizing and the self-repairing behavior of molecules are exploited in the design of computer networks [10]. The authors described the advantages of autonomic assembly of molecules and their application in computing. Habib and Marimuthu [11] presented a molecular assembly based network design tool to integrate the nodes in a given network into various clusters utilizing distance and traffic as forces of attractions. The authors claimed that the optimized and clustered network generated using the tool was able to reduce the backbone traffic. In an approach to estimate the carbon footprint the authors claimed that redesigning the existing network topology within Simulated Annealing enabled reduction in carbon emission [12][13].

In this work, we have utilized the molecular assembly to generate integrated clusters for a given set of nodes to comply with the standards of fiber-optic and Wi-Fi connectivity. We have carried out various experiments to explore the feasibility of the assembled network in reducing the utilization of network resources and CO_2 emission.

3   Capacity Planning through Molecular Assembly

We have utilized molecular assembly (MA) to perform a capacity planning on a fiber-optic enabled enterprise network as illustrated in Figure 1, wherein an enterprise network with a group of LANs utilizing Wi-Fi access points is connected through an optical switch at the backbone. The optical fiber switch offers 2 ports of 10/100Base-FX optical fiber and 24 ports of 10/100Base-Tx Copper in full-duplex mode and it supports STAR network topology [16]. The molecular assembly algorithm as illustrated in Figure 2 works in similarity with the molecular assembly in nature, which goes over sequentially to discover various patterns of node assembly with distance as the force of attraction. Further, it optimizes the generated clusters to reduce the backbone traffic.

The network parameters fed as inputs to the algorithm are S and T, whereby S represents a set of tuples of a computing node and its attributes such as node identifier and location and T denotes the traffic matrix that specifies the traffic between the individual nodes. In the MA algorithm, lines 2 to 4 generate the initial network assembly N and estimate the corresponding backbone traffic B and the carbon footprint C. Lines 8 to 11 recluster the initial network (N) with distance as the force of attraction and generates a new network assembly N^*. Subsequently, it computes the backbone traffic (B^*) and the volume of carbon emission (C^*). The distance threshold is selected to comply with the Wi-Fi standards. Lines 12 to 16 optimize the reclustered assembly by grouping the highly associated nodes together and quantify the amount of carbon emission. The performance of the generated system is compared with the previous system and the algorithm loops the optimization process to generate an optimized network. If it fails to generate optimized clusters, then it analyzes the set of generated clusters and if necessary, it restarts the procedure to rediscover the pattern exist among the nodes.

4   Network Problem Description

The suitability of the given enterprise network in delivering the data with reduced CO_2 and with reduced usage of resources at the backbone-level is analyzed through the proposed molecular assembly. The initial network is a single clustered network comprised of a set of tuples, $S = \{(n_1,l_1), (n_2,l_2), (n_3,l_3), ..., (n_M, l_M)\}$ distributed in a given 2-dimensional area A, where M represents the total number of nodes present. We have utilized the distance force to generate clusters within the network.

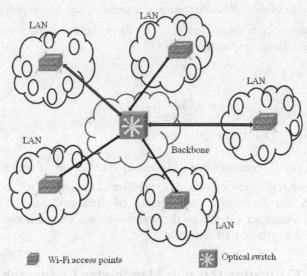

Fig. 1. A generic enterprise network model

```
Molecular-Assembly(S,T)

1. begin

2.   N = Create-single-cluster-assembly(S,T);
3.   B = estimate-backbone-traffic(N)
4.   C = estimate-CO₂-emission(B);
5.   If (B and C are not acceptable)
6.    While (terminating conditions unsatisfied) do
7.     begin
8.        Examine-forces-between-all-nodes(S);
9.        N* = reclustered-assembly utilizing-
              distance force-among node-pairs(N);
10.        B* = estimate-backbone-traffic(N*)
11.        C* = estimate-CO₂-emission(B*);
12.          If (all-node-assembled-into-clusters)
13.          O = optimized assembly-subject-to
                inter-cluster-node-movement(N*);
14.            B**= estimate-backbone-traffic(O)
15.            C** = estimate-CO₂-emission(B**);
16.          else go back to step 8;
17.       If (value of(C** and B**)acceptable)
18.        stop the algorithm;
19.       else go back to step 12;
20.     End;
21.   End;
```

Fig. 2. Capacity planning through molecular assembly

The physical Euclidian distance between a node n_i and any other node n_j in the given set of tuples in S forms the distance force between the two nodes and is governed by the following Quantifiers (1-3).

Initially $C_k = \{\ \}$ 　　　　　　　　　　　　　　　　　　　　　　　(1)

$\forall n_i, n_j$ and $n_i, n_j \in S$ and $i \neq j, \exists DF\ (l_i, l_j) > 0$ 　　　　　　　　(2)

$C_k = \{C_k \cup \{n_i, n_j\} | DF(l_i, l_j)\} \geq DF\_threshold$ 　　　　　　　　　(3)

Here the Quantifier (1) indicates that a cluster C_k starts empty of nodes. The subscript k specifies the identification of cluster. Quantifier (2) examines all distinct pairwise nodes within S and determines the existence of distance force (DF) between the selected nodes. Quantifier (3) groups the nodes within a cluster if the distance force (DF) satisfies the threshold (| DF_threshold |).

5   Power Estimation through Manchester Coding for Green Communications

We have derived a procedure to estimate the power consumed by the data flow at the backbone, as green communication is ensured from reduced power consumption. We have selected Manchester NRZ signaling to code the backbone data, as it uses less bandwidth to transport data. The power spectral density (PSD) for a line code can be evaluated using the stochastic approach. The power spectral density for Manchester NRZ signal with unit amplitude and rectangular pulse is represented by Equation (4). Here the bit rate (BR) is given by $1/T_b$ [14].

$$P_{Manchester-NRZ}(f) = T_b \left(\frac{\sin(\pi f\ T_b/2)}{\pi f\ T_b/2} \right)^2 \sin^2(\pi f\ T_b/2) \tag{4}$$

The area under the PSD function is the normalized power [13] and is represented by Equation (5).

$$P = \langle w^2(t) \rangle = \int_{-\infty}^{\infty} P_w(f) df \tag{5}$$

We have derived an equation to estimate an equivalent volume of CO_2 emission utilizing the power computed from Equation (5). Let E be the energy consumed per day in transmitting the encoded data, represented as E in watt-hour. The amount of CO_2 released per day during the data communications is computed using Equation (6). The conversion factor to convert energy into CO_2 for fuel oil is 0.282 [15].

Amount of CO_2 emission per day $= A_{CO_2} = E * 0.282$ 　　　　　　　　(6)

6   Results and Discussion

We have considered a medium scale enterprise network comprising of 60 nodes deployed as a single cluster network, with backbone traffic of around 1.2 Gbits/sec. We have applied the proposed molecular assembly algorithm to analyze the capacity planning of resources, whereby the enterprise is converted into a multi-clustered network. The MA algorithm starts exploring the given network with distance as a force of attraction and the distance force threshold is varied up to 100 meters to simulate the real time Wi-Fi scenario.

We have carried out two sets of experiments within MA to reduce CO_2 emission, wherein the first experiment employs a distance force threshold of 80 meters and the second experiment is tested with a threshold of 100 meters. The reclustering and the optimization phases of MA for a distance threshold of 80 meters are illustrated in Figure 3. It is observed from Figure 3 that the MA algorithm manages to reduce the number of clusters from 25 to 5, thus facilitating the usage of fiber optic switch with reduced ports. The optimized movement of highly associated nodes together into a single cluster from their parent clusters reduces the backbone traffic, thereby reduces the bandwidth utilization of the fiber-optic cable at the backbone by 26%. Moreover, the local traffic within the generated clusters of 80 meters radius varies from 787 kilobits/sec to 1.56 Mbits/sec, thus supporting reduced number of Wi-Fi access points within each cluster. However, with a distance threshold of 100 meters as illustrated in Figure 3, the numbers of clusters are reduced from 25 to 3 and the local traffic within the generated clusters of 100 meters radius varies from 820 Kbits/sec to 3.03 Mbits/sec. The reduction in the backbone traffic is around 43%, thereby generating provision for network scalability.

6.1   Evaluating the Performance through CO_2 Emission

The power spectral density (PSD) for the given network as illustrated in Figure 4 is estimated using the theory of power calculation with Manchester digital encoding schemes. In Figure 4, the estimated power spectral density values are normalized for the given traffic, whereby the traffic is represented in bits/sec. It is observed from the PSD graph that the optimized network generated utilizing MA occupies lesser band of frequencies than the initial network, thus consuming lesser bandwidth and lesser time to transmit. The total normalized power consumed for the selected data transmission is estimated by integrating the area under the corresponding power spectral density curve as given by Equation (5). Table I summarizes the amount of power consumed, and the corresponding CO_2 for the generated traffic volumes at the backbone. The energy consumed in kW per day, presented in column 3 is calculated by considering the data transmission for 8 hours per day and 365 days per year. It is observed that the multi-clustered network reduced the CO_2 emission by 53% on comparison with the initial network.

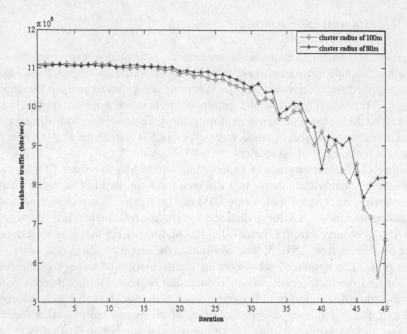

Fig. 3. Comparison of behavior of MA with various distance thresholds

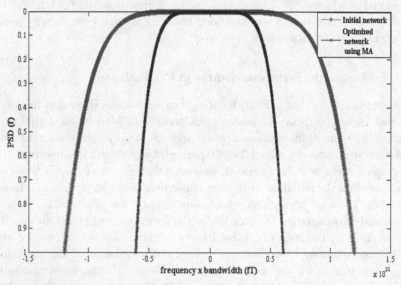

Fig. 4. Power spectral density of various traffic volumes at the backbone for a distance threshold of 100 meters

Table 1. Carbon footprint estimation

Network	Back-bone traffic (Gbits/sec)	Power consumed per day (kW)	CO_2 per year (metric ton)
Initial network (Single clustered)	1.2	54.1	5.5
network utilizing MA (Multi-clustered)	0.63	25.2	2.59

7 Conclusion

We have employed a molecular assembly scheme within a capacity planning tool to facilitate green communications in an enterprise network, whereby the MA discovers the set of associated nodes and it integrates them together to generate a clustered enterprise network. The distance threshold is varied in accordance with the communication limit of Wi-Fi connectivity to facilitate Wi-Fi access points for local communication. The performance evaluation by estimating the amount of CO_2 released from the generated backbone traffic shows an annual reduction of 53% than the initial network.

References

1. Mohamed, A.A., ElHalawany, M.E., Rashed, A.N.Z., ElNabawy, A.E.M.: Transmission Performance Analysis of Digital Wire and Wireless Optical Links in Local and Wide Areas Optical Networks. International Journal of Computer Science and Information Security 3(1) (2009)
2. Sidhu, B., Singh, H., Chhabra, A.: Emerging Wireless Standards- WiFi, Zigbee and WiMax. World Academy of Science, Engineering and Technology 25, 308–313 (2007)
3. Habib, S.J., Marimuthu, P.N.: Self-organization in Ambient Networks through Molecular Assembly. Journal of Ambient Intelligence and Humanized Computing 2, 165–173 (2011)
4. Ross Ashby, W.: Principles of Self-Organizing System. Emergence: Complexity & Organization 6(1-2), 102–126 (2004)
5. Raghunath, S., Ramakrishnan, K.K.: Trade-offs in Resource Management for Virtual Private Networks. In: IEEE INFOCOM, Miami, USA, March 13-17 (2005)
6. Gmach, D., Rollia, J., Cherkasova, L., Kemper, A.: Workload Analysis and Demand Prediction of Enterprise Data Center Applications. In: IEEE Int. Symposium on Workload Characterization, Boston, MA, USA, September 27-29 (2007)
7. Chiaraviglio, L., Mellia, M., Neri, F.: Energy-aware Backbone Networks: a Case Study. In: The Proceedings of First International Workshop on Green Communications, Dresden, Germany, June 14-18 (2009)
8. Yang, W., Kang, D., Tong, F., Kim, Y.: Performance Analysis of Energy Savings according to Traffic Patterns in Ethernet with Rate Adaptation. In: 12th International Conference on Computer Modeling and Simulation, Cambridge, UK, March 24-26, pp. 619–624 (2010)

9. Vereecken, W., Heddeghem, W.V., Colle, D., Pickavet, M., Demeester, P.: Overall ICT Footprint and Green Communication Technologies. In: 4th International Symposium on Communications, Control and Signal Processing, Limassol, Cyprus, March 3-5 (2010)
10. Gershenson, C., Heylighen, F.: When Can We Call a System Self-Organizing? In: Banzhaf, W., Ziegler, J., Christaller, T., Dittrich, P., Kim, J.T. (eds.) ECAL 2003. LNCS (LNAI), vol. 2801, pp. 606–614. Springer, Heidelberg (2003)
11. Habib, S.J., Marimuthu, P.N.: Molecular Assembly Tool for Synthesizing Multi-tier Computer Networks. In: 23rd IEEE International Conference on Tools with Artificial Intelligence, Boca Raton, Florida, USA, November 7-9 (2003) (Poster)
12. Habib, S.J., Marimuthu, P.N.: Carbon Offsetting through Computer Network Redesign. In: International Conference on Information Networking 2012, Bali, Indonesia, February 1-3 (2012) (Poster)
13. Habib, S.J., Marimuthu, P.N., Zaeri, N.: Green Communications through Network Redesign. In: Abraham, A., Lloret Mauri, J., Buford, J.F., Suzuki, J., Thampi, S.M. (eds.) ACC 2011. CCIS, vol. 191, pp. 349–357. Springer, Heidelberg (2011)
14. Couch II, L.W.: Digital and Analog Communication Systems, Pearson International edn., USA (2007)
15. Carbon Footprint Conversion Factors, http://archive.defra.gov.uk/environment/business/reporting/pdf/101006-guidelines-ghg-conversion-factors.pdf
16. Optical Switches, http://www.smartoptics.com

Energy Consumption of Wireless Network Access Points

Sebastián Andrade-Morelli, Eduardo Ruiz-Sánchez,
Emilio Granell, and Jaime Lloret

Universidad Politécnica de Valencia,
Camino Vera s/n, 46022, Valencia, Spain
{seanmo,edruisan}@epsg.upv.es,
emgraro@posgrado.upv.es, jlloret@dcom.upv.es

Abstract. The development of low cost technology based on IEEE 802.11 standard permits to build telecommunication networks at low cost, allowing providing Internet access in rural areas in developing countries. The lack of access to the electrical grid is a problem when the network is being developed in rural areas, so that wireless access points should operate using solar panels and batteries. Many cases can be found where the energy consumption becomes a key point in wireless network design. In this paper we present a comparative study of the energy consumption of several wireless network access points. We will compare the energy consumption of different brands and models, for several operation scenarios and operating modes. Obtained results allow us to achieve the objective of this article, that is, promote the development of wireless communication networks energetically efficient.

Keywords: Energy consumption, Power Consumption, Access Points, Green Networks, Smart Grid.

1   Introduction

In recent years, the network devices have evolved to improve network performance [1]. These improvements are also happening in wireless network devices reducing its economical cost. The development of low cost technology based on IEEE 802.11 [2] has facilitated the development of applications for monitoring natural areas through wireless sensor networks (WSN) [3] and the development of data networks for Internet access for end users.

The popularization of mobile devices allowing wireless access to networks is motivating the municipalities to provide an independent community network to provide different services to citizens [4].

Furthermore, this type of community networks can offer all kinds of applications for-profit and not-for-profit [5]. The municipalities can use these networks to promote its economical development, offering applications for business and tourism to citizens. At the same time, these networks can be used for remote monitoring of parking meters and street lights even the automation of other services [6]. Nowadays, wireless access devices can just change the data link layer, acting as a wireless access point, or even route between networks, where several common routing protocols can be configured [7].

J. Lloret Mauri and J.J.P.C. Rodrigues (Eds.): GreeNets 2012, LNICST 113, pp. 81–91, 2013.
© Institute for Computer Sciences, Social Informatics and Telecommunications Engineering 2013

Wireless networks offer the possibility to build telecommunications networks at low cost, allowing providing Internet access in rural areas in developing countries [8]. The lack of access to the electrical grid is a problem when the network is being developing in rural areas. One possible solution to this problem is to power network access points using solar panels and batteries, so its power consumption becomes a key issue to ensure its operation [9]. Moreover, some researchers are proposing new intelligent algorithms for the MAC layer that improve the performance of the network [10] and, thus, reduce the energy consumption of the wireless devices [11].

In this paper, we present a study of the energy consumption in wireless access points, depending on the brand, model and its configuration. With this study we also sought to determine if the wireless technology and frequency band used affect energy usage in the access point. These measures will serve as a tool for designing energy efficient wireless networks.

The rest of the paper is structured as follows, Section 2 shows several previous works and researches regarding to consumption and saving energy in wireless access points. In Section 3 are shown the topologies and the description of the characteristics of the access points used to perform these tests. The obtained measurement results and the discussion are shown in Section 4. Finally, the conclusions and future works are shown in Section 5.

2   Related Work

Currently, there is a great interest in the analysis of the power consumption of network devices because ecological and economical reasons. L.M. Feeney et al. in [12] present a study about the energy consumption of wireless networks interfaces in ad-hoc networks. Several authors have focused their analysis on energy consumption from the point of view of the development of software tools. In [13] the authors present intelligent equipment allowing the energy saving, using smart routing. These tools intend to control the consumption of wireless networks. Another example is the work presented in [14], where T. Chen et al. proposed a series of strategies for achieving or at least approaching the goals of establishing a "green network", these solutions are based on the correct choice of the IEEE 802.11 standard, as well as the different devices to form Wireless Networks.

S. Sendra et al. present in [15] different techniques for saving energy in wireless sensor networks. The paper shows how a sensor node must be and the relationship between the quantity of information transmitted and the power consumption by the hardware used. Authors have also compared several MAC and routing protocols that have been designed to optimize the power consumption without compromising the data delivery in wireless sensor and ah-hoc networks.

But as far as we know there is no study focused on the energy consumption of wireless access points from the point of view of their model and their configuration. With our work we want to offer a tool for developing and maintaining wireless telecommunications networks energetically efficient. So the study presented in this paper serves as a reference both to the development of wireless networks in rural areas of developing countries and to reduce consumption in wireless networks in general.

3   Scenarios and Hardware Description

In order to carry out our measurements, we need to test the performance of multiple access points of different brands and models. In this section we will see the technical characteristics of the selected devices for our study and describe the topologies used to fulfil our measurements. To measure the energy consumption, we used an electronic device called "Kill a Watt". This device is able to measure the electrical voltage, current and power parameters with 1% of measurement error.

We need different network topologies to compare how affect to wireless access points energy consumption all its configurable parameters, especially, when we compare energy consumption between a completely wireless network and a half-wired network. Figure 1 shows the two topologies used to carry out our study. On one hand in the Topology 1, the access point is used to connect two endpoints, the first one with a wireless connection and the second one with a wired connection, in the other hand in Topology 2, the access point is used to connect two endpoints with wireless connections.

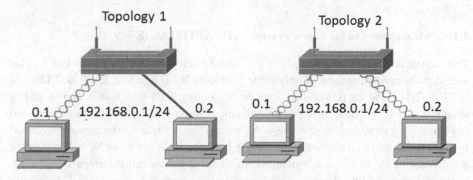

Fig. 1. Network topologies

Table 1 shows wireless network access points used in our study and their relevant characteristics.

Table 1. Wireless network access points and its relevant characteristics

	Frequency band (Ghz)	Operating temperature (°C)	Internal memory (MB)	Flash memory (MB)	Max data transfer rate (Mbps)	Wireless protocol	Data transmission protocol
Cisco Systems AIR-AP1131AG-E-K9	2.4	0-40	32	16	108	IEEE 802.11a/b/g	Fast Ethernet
Cisco Linksys WRT54GL	2.4	0-40	16	4	54	IEEE 802.11b/g	Ethernet, Fast Ethernet
Cisco Linksys WRT320N-EZ	2.4/5.0	0-40	32	8	300	IEEE 802.11b/g/a/n	Ethernet, Fast Ethernet
D-link DWL-2000Ap+	2.4	0-55	16	4	54	IEEE 802.11b/g	Ethernet, Fast Ethernet
Avaya AP-I	2.4	0-40	16	4	11	IEEE 802.11b	Ethernet
Ovislink WX-1590	2.4	0-55	16	4	11	IEEE 802.11b	Ethernet

For each wireless access point we define two different measurement cases:

- First case: the measure of energy consumed at starting state and at steady state.
- Second case: the measure of energy consumed for both topologies, for each wireless protocol and frequency band permitted by the access point:

    o   For sending an echo from PC 1 to PC 2.
    o   For sending a file of 2.45 GB from PC 1 to PC 2.

4   Result of Measurements

After configuring the different wireless access points we have tested it using both topologies. The energy measurements obtained from the tests are shown in several tables and graphs with the goal of compare their values. With these comparatives we will determine which access point consumes less energy, and how affect the different parameters to energy consumption.

4.1   Measurements for Cisco Systems AIR-AP1131AG-E-K9

The first access point under study is a Cisco Systems AIR-AP1131AG-E-K9. This access point can be configured only using protocols IEEE 802.11a, IEEE 802.11b and IEEE 802.11g and its power consumption at starting state is 5.1 W·h and at steady state is 5.4 W·h. In Table 2 we present the values of power consumption in case 2 and in Figure 2 we represent these values. As we can see in Figure 2 the power consumed by this device during transmission is always between 10 W·h and 11 W·h. We observe an increase of 2% in power consumption in air-air communication compared with air-cable communication. We can also see how the protocol IEEE 802.11b usually consumes less energy except in the case of sending a file in the topology 1. Finally, the increase of power consumption for activation of the MAC filter is confirmed as expected, in this case becomes 2%.

Table 2. Measurements for the second case

	Power consumption (W.h)					
	IEEE 802.11a	IEEE 802.11b	IEEE 802.11g	IEEE 802.11a with MAC filter	IEEE 802.11b with MAC filter	IEEE 802.11g with MAC filter
Topology 1						
Sending echo	10.3	10.2	10.2	10.4	10.2	10.3
Sending file	10.5	10.5	10.4	10.7	10.6	10.4
Topology 2						
Sending echo	10.4	10.3	10.3	10.4	103	10.4
Sending file	10.7	10.5	10.6	10.7	10.5	10.7

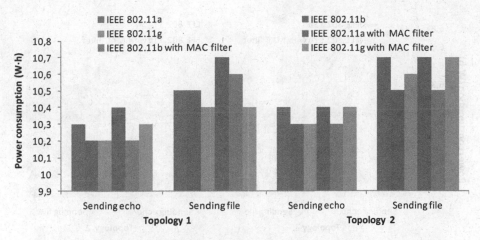

Fig. 2. Power consumption for second case for Cisco Systems AIR-AP1131AG-E-K9

4.2   Measurements for Cisco Linksys WRT54GL

The second access point that we will discuss is a Cisco Linksys WRT54GL. This access point allows only protocols IEEE 802.11b and IEEE 802.11g and its power consumption is 5.2 W·h at starting state and 5.7 W·h at steady state. In Table 3 are shown the values of power consumption obtained for the second case of measurements and in Figure 3 its representation. As we can observe in Figure 3, the energy consumed by this access point is considerably less than the consumed by the previous model. This model consumes around 40% less energy. From the obtained values, is observed for this device that IEEE 802.11g protocol consumes less energy than IEEE 802.11b protocol, and as in the previous model, the activation of the MAC filter increase the energy consumption, the air-air transmission consume more energy that the air-cable transmission and sending a file also consume more than sending an echo.

Table 3. Measurements for the second case

	Power consumption (W·h)			
	IEEE 802.11b	IEEE 802.11g	IEEE 802.11b with MAC filter	IEEE 802.11g with MAC filter
Topology 1				
Sending echo	6	6	6.1	6.2
Sending file	6.2	6.1	6.2	6.2
Topology 2				
Sending echo	6	6.1	6.1	6.1
Sending file	6.4	6.3	6.5	6.3

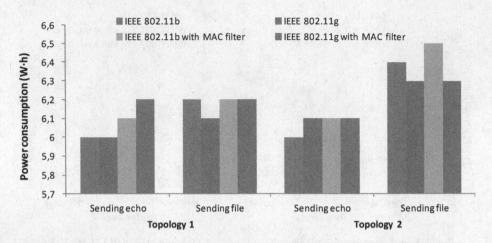

Fig. 3. Power consumption for second case for Cisco Linksys WRT54GL

4.3   Measurements for Cisco Linksys WRT320N-EZ

In this case we will analyse the energy consumption of the access point Cisco Linksys WRT320N-EZ. This device consumes 4.5 W·h at starting state and 4.8 W·h at steady state. The values of the energy consumed for the second case of measurements is shown in Table 4 and in Figure 4 are represented this values. This access point allows the protocols IEEE 802.11a, IEEE 802.11b, IEEE 802.11g and IEEE 802.11n. As we can see, this device consumes less energy than the previously studied. We note that the IEEE 802.11n protocol is the one that consumes less energy but there is two cases in which consumes 1% more energy than IEEE 802.11g. We observed the same effect previously regarding the activation of the MAC filter comparing topologies and type of communication.

Table 4. Measurements for the second case

	\multicolumn{8}{c}{Power consumption (W·h)}							
	IEEE 802.11a	IEEE 802.11b	IEEE 802.11g	IEEE 802.11n	IEEE 802.11a with MAC filter	IEEE 802.11b with MAC filter	IEEE 802.11g with MAC filter	IEEE 802.11n with MAC filter
Topology 1								
Sending echo	5.3	5.3	5.2	5.3	5.3	5.3	5.3	5.3
Sending file	5.4	5.4	5.4	5.3	5.5	5.5	5.4	5.4
Topology 2								
Sending echo	5.3	5.3	5.3	5.3	5.4	5.3	5.3	5.4
Sending file	5.5	5.6	5.5	5.4	5.5	5.7	5.6	5.5

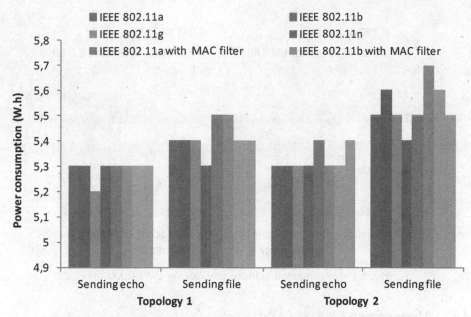

Fig. 4. Power consumption for second case for Cisco Linksys WRT320N-EZ

4.4   Measurements for D-link DWL-2000Ap+

The fourth case analyses the consumption of the access point D-Link Access Point DWL 2000AP. The power consumption in the first case of measurement for this device is 3.4 W·h at starting state and 4.8 W·h at steady state. This access point allows only protocols IEEE 802.11b and IEEE 802.11g. In Table 5 are shown the values of power consumption obtained for the second case of measurements and in Figure 5 its representation. As we can observe in Figure 5, the energy consumed by this access point is considerably less than the consumed by Cisco models. This device consumes approximately 16% less energy than the model of Cisco (Cisco Linksys WRT54GL) offering the same services. In this device IEEE 802.11b protocol consumes less energy than IEEE 802.11g protocol, but respect to extra consumption generated by the MAC filter, by the second topology and the transmission of a file, the conclusions are the same as in the previous access points.

Table 5. Measurements for the second case

	Power consumption (W·h)			
	IEEE 802.11b	IEEE 802.11g	IEEE 802.11b with MAC filter	IEEE 802.11g with MAC filter
Topology 1				
Sending echo	5	5.1	5.1	5.2
Sending file	5.1	5.2	5.2	5.2
Topology 2				
Sending echo	5.1	5.1	5.2	5.2
Sending file	5.3	5.3	5.4	5.4

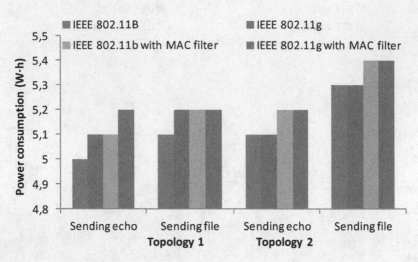

Fig. 5. Power consumption for second case for DWL-2000Ap+

4.5   Measurements for Avaya AP-I

The fifth case analyses the consumption of the access point Avaya Access Point I. The capabilities of this access point are more limited compared with the previous ones and its consumption is 2.8 W·h at starting state and 3.2 W·h at steady state. This device allows only protocol IEEE 802.11b. In Table 6 are shown the values of power consumption obtained for the second case of measurements and in Figure 6 its representation. As we can see in Figure 6 this device consumes less energy than the previous ones, an explanation for this fact is its limited hardware. In this device the increase in the energy consumed introduced by the use of the MAC filter is approximately 3%. For the rest of parameters studied, we observe the same behaviour observed on the rest of access points.

Table 6. Measurements for the second case

	Power consumption (W·h)	
	IEEE 802.11b	IEEE 802.11b with MAC filter
Topology 1		
Sending echo	3.2	3.3
Sending file	3.4	3.5
Topology 2		
Sending echo	3.3	3.4
Sending file	3.5	3.5

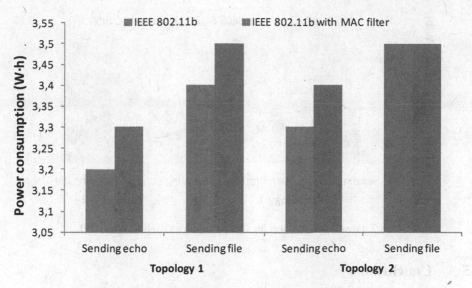

Fig. 6. Power consumption for second case for Avaya AP-I

4.6   Measurements for Ovislink WX-1590

The sixth case analyses the consumption of the Ovislink Access point WX-1590. This access point has limited capabilities as the previous one, but this device consumes around 40% more energy. Its consumption is 4.8 W·h at starting state and 5.4W·h at steady state. This device allows only protocol IEEE 802.11b.

Table 7 shows the values of power consumption obtained for the second case of measurements and Fig. 7 shows its representation. For the rest of studied parameters, we observe the same behaviour observed on the rest of access points.

Table 7. Measurements for the second case

	Power consumption (W·h)	
	IEEE 802.11b	IEEE 802.11b with MAC filter
Topology 1		
Sending echo	5.5	5.4
Sending file	5.5	5.5
Topology 2		
Sending echo	5.5	5.6
Sending file	6	6.2

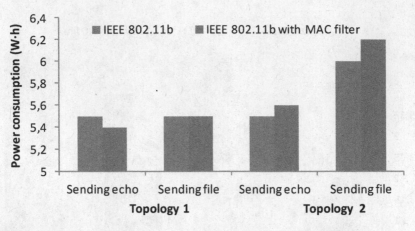

Fig. 7. Power consumption for second case for Ovislink WX-1590

5   Conclusions

In this paper we present a study on energy consumption in wireless access points. We have measured the energy consumption at the starting and steady states. We also measured the energy when there are devices sending echoes and files between them through the access point and with the MAC filter is active and disabled in two different network topologies. In our study we have shown that energy consumption increases in all studied models when MAC filter is enabled, sending a file and when the communication between computers is air to air. We have also seen that models with higher capabilities consume more energy than models with reduced capabilities. The results of this study demonstrate that it is possible to optimize the energy efficiency of the network using the access point models and parameters suitable to the requirements of the network. These factors are very important in places where power consumption is critical.

In future work, we will extend our study to other telecommunication network devices such as routers and switches. The choice of network devices is a key issue in energy savings in telecommunication networks, so with these studies we sought to determine which devices and their configuration are more suitable for the development of green communications networks.

References

[1] Khoa Nguyen, K., Jaumard, B.: Routing Engine Architecture for Next Generation Routers: Evolutional Trends. Network Protocols and Algorithms 1(1), 62–85 (2009)
[2] IEEE Std 802.11: IEEE Standard for Information technology -Telecommunications and information exchange between systems -Local and metropolitan area networks - Specific requirements – Part 11: Wireless LAN Medium Access Control (MAC) and Physical Layer (PHY) Specifications. Institute of Electrical and Electronics Engineers, New York, USA, pp.1–1184 (2007)

[3] Lloret, J., Garcia, M., Bri, D., Sendra, S.: A Wireless Sensor Network Deployment for Rural and Forest Fire Detection and Verification. Sensors 9(11), 8722–8747 (2009)

[4] Tapia, A., Maitland, C., Stone, M.: Making IT work for Municipalities: Building municipal wireless networks. Government Information Quarterly 23(3), 359–380 (2006)

[5] van Drunen, R., Koolhaas, J., Schuurmans, H., Vijn, M.: Building a Wireless Community Network in the Netherland. In: USENIX 2003 / Freenix Annual Technical Conference Proceedings, San Antonio, Texas, USA, June 9-14, pp. 219–230 (2003)

[6] Powell, A., Shade, L.R.: Going Wi-Fi in Canada: Municipal and Community Initiatives. Canadian Research Alliance for Community Innovation and Networking (2005)

[7] Sendra, S., Fernández, P.A., Quilez, M.A., Lloret, J.: Study and Performance of Interior Gateway IP routing Protocols. Network Protocols and Algorithms 2(4), 88–117 (2010)

[8] Galperin, H.: Wireless Networks and Rural Development: Opportunities for Latin America. Information Technologies and International Development 2(3), 47–56 (2005)

[9] Segal, M.: Improving lifetime of wireless sensor networks. Network Protocols and Algorithms 1(2), 48–60 (2009)

[10] Momani, A.A.E., Yassein, M.B., Darwish, O., Manaseer, S., Mardini, W.: Intelligent Paging Backoff Algorithm for IEEE 802.11 MAC Protocol. Network Protocols and Algorithms 4(2), 108–123 (2012)

[11] Mohsin, A.H., Bakar, K.A., Adekiigbe, A., Ghafoor, K.Z.: A Survey of Energy-aware Routing protocols in Mobile Ad-hoc Networks: Trends and Challenges. Network Protocols and Algorithms 4(2), 82–107 (2012)

[12] Feeney, L.M., Nilsson, M.: Investigating the Energy Consumption of a Wireless Network Interface in an Ad Hoc Networking Environment. In: Proceedings of the Twentieth Annual Joint Conference of the IEEE Computer and Communications Societies, INFOCOM 2001, Anchorage, Alaska, April 22-26, vol. 3, pp. 1548–1557. IEEE (2001)

[13] Barbancho, J., León, C., Molina, F.J., Barbancho, A.: Using artificial intelligence in routing schemes for wireless networks. Computer Communications 30(14-15), 2802–2811 (2007)

[14] Tao, C., Yang, Y., Honggang, Z., Haesik, K., Horneman, K.: Network energy saving technologies for green wireless access networks. IEEE Wireless Communications 18(5), 30–38 (2011)

[15] Sendra, S., Lloret, J., Garcia, M., Toledo, J.F.: Power saving and energy optimization techniques for Wireless Sensor Networks. Journal of Communications 6(6), 439–459 (2011)

Astroparticle Physics and Green Communication and Networking: A Symbiosis

Miguel Ardid

Universitat Politècnica de València,
Institut d'Investigació per a la Gestió Integrada de Zones Costaneres (IGIC)
Paranimf 1, 46730 Gandia, Spain
mardid@fis.upv.es

Abstract. In this paper, the links between astroparticle physics and green communication and networking are described. Due to the advanced scientific and technological frame and the need of green networking that the astroparticle facilities and experiments have, good synergies between both fields can appear. Examples of these synergies of using green networking and communication technologies in deep-sea neutrino telescopes (such as the data acquisition and communication systems of ANTARES, and the KM3NeT acoustic positioning and monitoring system) are also presented.

Keywords: Astroparticle Physics, Sensor Networks, Green Communication and Networking, Neutrino Telescopes.

1 Introduction

Astroparticle Physics (ApP) is a field of research emerging at the intersection of particle physics, astronomy, and cosmology. It aims to answer fundamental questions related to the Universe such as: What is the Universe made of? What is dark matter and dark energy? What is the origin of cosmic rays? What is the nature of gravity? What has been the evolution of the Universe?, etc. To answer these very challenging questions, physicists are developing experiments to detect messengers from the Universe. In 1912 Hess demonstrated that there was radiation coming from the sky studying the ionization as a function of height using a balloon (ApP is celebrating the century of life). From then on, in addition to the ancient astronomy which uses visible light, new messengers (the whole electromagnetic wave spectrum, cosmic rays and neutrinos) are used to get complementary information to increase our understanding of the Universe.

2 Links between Astroparticle Physics and Green Communication and Networking

Experiments and data communication in ApP is probably the more demanding field in data acquisition, communication and networking aspects in the most varied situations,

J. Lloret Mauri and J.J.P.C. Rodrigues (Eds.): GreeNets 2012, LNICST 113, pp. 92–101, 2013.
© Institute for Computer Sciences, Social Informatics and Telecommunications Engineering 2013

some of them in very adverse environments and with serious constrains of power availability and data transmission. We can realize it in examples, such as ANTARES[1] and KM3NeT[2] deep-sea neutrino telescopes. In these facilities, thousands of optical sensors and other instrumentation monitor synchronously at the nanosecond level large volumes of water in order to search for signals from high energy neutrinos and discriminate them from a much larger optical background. Due to the location (at sea and few kilometers depth), there are serious constrains in terms of power and communication transmission. A large effort is being made to overcome these difficulties that results in efficient systems and techniques that are promising advances in green communication and networking.

The situation is not very different in other ApP experiments, such as neutrino telescopes in deep-ice in the Antarctica (Icecube[3]), very large arrays to detect ultra-high energy cosmic rays (Auger[4]) or gammas (CTA[5]), also in the space (Fermi[6], JEM-Euso[7]). The situation is even more demanding with new initiatives, such as the Global Neutrino Observatory or the Astrophysical Multimessenger Observatory Network, which tries to distribute data and information between different ApP experiments and other astrophysical telescopes distributed all over the world, both online and off-line, to enhance the potential of discoveries and understanding of the Universe. Data must be handled, processed fast and efficiently distributed over thousands of scientists and engineers for a right analysis, keeping into consideration aspects such as confidentiality, right levels, etc.

On the other hand, research in Green Communication and Networking (GCN) technologies results in new tools to reduce power consumption and increase efficiency in networking by means of energy-efficient sensors, protocols, transmission technologies, cross-layer optimizations, peer-to-peer networking, cloud computing, hardware and architectural support and network management techniques. GCN also aims advances in renewable energy sources for wired and wireless access networks.

Due to the large need in communications and networking in ApP facilities and experiments, and the constrains in terms of power and infrastructure due to their locations, advances in GCN technologies are of great use in ApP in order to increase the potential of ongoing experiments and design the future ones. Therefore, ApP can be a very good partner and customer for new developments in this area.

3   Example case: Deep Sea Neutrino Telescopes and Links with Green Communications and Networking

Neutrino telescopes provide a new and unique method to observe the Universe, so they will open a new window on it. Deep sea neutrino telescopes in the Mediterranean

---

[1] http://antares.in2p3.fr
[2] http://km3net.org
[3] http://icecube.wisc.edu
[4] http://www.auger.org
[5] http://www.cta-observatory.org
[6] http://fermi.gsfc.nasa.gov
[7] http://jemeuso.riken.jp/en

Sea are either in operation, case of ANTARES [1,2], or in the construction Phase, case of KM3NeT [3,4].

The ANTARES (Astronomy with a Neutrino Telescope and Abyss environmental RESearch) Collaboration has built a large effective area water Cherenkov detector in the deep Mediterranean Sea optimised for the detection of muons from high-energy astrophysical neutrinos. It is, at present, the largest neutrino telescope in the northern hemisphere and the largest underwater neutrino telescope in the world. This facility has represented a technological challenge since a large amount of sensors of different kinds had to be deployed and connected in deep sea to become a network of coordinated underwater sensors looking for neutrinos and monitoring the deep sea. The telescope is based on the reconstruction of the trajectory and energy of neutrinos by detecting the Cherenkov light from muons, which are particles produced in some neutrino interactions. Since the neutrino interaction probability is extremely low (it could pass right through Earth without even noticing), only some of them will interact. In order to have a reasonable number of events a huge sensitive volume of detection is required. On the other hand, the presence of other cosmic rays, which are more abundant and with larger interaction probabilities than neutrinos, will completely mask neutrino signals. In order to avoid this situation, a large shield of kilometres of water is necessary to stop other cosmic rays than neutrinos and make the telescope feasible. This is the reason for the particular location of the ANTARES telescope: 2500 m deep in the Mediterranean Sea, 40 km off shore from Toulon (France).

To make this idea feasible a detector with an effective surface area of about 0.1 km^2 composed of 12 vertical lines of about 450 m height and about 70 m spacing, holding nearly 900 photomultipliers has been built and deployed. Besides the Optical Module (OM) sensors, a set of calibration sensors (optical beacons, acoustic transducers, tiltmeters and compasses), a data acquisition system and communication networks are needed. A specific dedicated instrumentation line with multidisciplinary oceanographic equipment and acoustic sensors have been deployed as well. All this configure a large interrelated network of systems of sensors looking for neutrinos and monitoring the deep sea.

ANTARES has the objective to detect and study very high-energy cosmic neutrino sources. Results from the telescope could produce a valuable insight not only in astronomy and astrophysics, but in particle physics, dark matter and cosmology as well. In addition, ANTARES houses instrumentation from other sciences like marine biology and geophysics for long term and on-line monitoring of the deep sea environment.

On the other side, The KM3NeT neutrino telescope can be understood as the next generation of this kind of neutrino telescopes with an instrumented volume larger than one cubic kilometer. For this, and according to [4], an array of optical sensors will be installed on several hundred vertical structures, the detection units (DUs), anchored on the seafloor and held taut by buoys. The DUs will be located at a distance of 180 m from each other. Each DU will consist of 20 horizontal bars (storeys) of 6 m length, with a vertical separation of 40 m between storeys. Two Digital Optical Modules (DOMs) are mounted in each storey. The DOM consists of 31 three-inch photomultipliers housed on a 17" glass sphere which also hosts read-out and data transmission electronics. An electro-optical submarine cable network, initiated from the shore station and split with primary and secondary junction boxes, will be used for distributing the electrical power, for control, and for managing the acquired data. Sea bottom connections between the detection units and the cable network will be carried out with deep-sea remotely operated vehicles. The overall power consumption of the telescope will be approximately 125 kW and the expected data rate will be roughly 25GBytes/s. For managing the large data stream to shore, a point-to-point fibre optic network transferring all the DOM data to the shore will be used. On the other hand, the shore station will house the power supplies, the lasers that will drive the fibre optic network, and will also host the data acquisition system that will implement data filtering, recording and distribution.

Next, we present some items of these telescopes where GCN technologies have had or will have a very relevant role.

3.1   Data Acquisition and Communication Systems of ANTARES

In order to handle all data coming from the underwater sensors of the ANTARES telescope, intelligent data acquisition (DAQ) and communication systems are required. The DAQ system of ANTARES is extensively described in [5]. Here, we summarise the main aspects of it. The photomultiplier signal is processed by the Analogue Ring Sampler (ARS), an ASIC card which digitizes the arrival time and charge of the pulse [6]. The readout trigger threshold of the ARS is set at about 0.3 photo-electrons. The OMs deliver their data in real time and can be remotely controlled from the ANTARES shore station through a Gb Ethernet network. Every storey is equipped with a Local Control Module containing the electronic boards for the OM signal processing, the instrument readout, the acoustic positioning, the power system and the data transmission. Every five storeys, in the middle, the Master Local Control Module (MLCM) also contains an Ethernet switch board, which multiplexes the DAQ channels from the other storeys. At the bottom of the line, the Bottom String Socket (BSS) is equipped with a String Control Module (SCM) which contains the local readout and DAQ electronics, as well as the power system for the whole line. Each of these containers constitutes a node of the data transmission network, receiving and transmitting data and slow-control commands. The functions supported by the SCM include reading sensors, adjusting slow-control parameters, the trigger, and the distribution of power, master clock and resetting signals to the front-end electronics. Finally, both MCLM and SCM include a Dense Wavelength Division Multiplexing system used for data transmission in order to merge several 1Gb/s Ethernet channels on the same pair of optical fibres, using different laser wavelengths.

The individual SCMs are linked to a common junction box by electro-optical cables which are connected using a ROV. A standard deep sea telecommunication cable links the junction box with a shore station where the data are filtered and recorded.

All data, times and pulse amplitudes, are stored in memory. In order to provide an efficient transfer of the data, the memory is divided in buffers of 104 ms length (time slice). The starting times of the buffers on each of the storeys are synchronised. These buffers are transmitted via an Ethernet network to a farm of processors on shore where candidate events are filtered from the continuous data stream for further off line processing. Individual processors in the farm receive and process all buffers from the full detector associated with a single time slice. Following this philosophy, the trigger logic in the sea was planned to be as simple and flexible as possible. In the present scheme, all OMs are continuously read out and sent to shore. Once the OM signal is above the ARS threshold (Level 0 hit), which is set around 1/3 of the single photoelectron level (SPE), then the data filter on-shore farm look for a physics event by searching a set of correlated Level 1 hits, which corresponds either to local coincidences of Level 0 hits within 20ns or for a high amplitude hit (typically > 3 SPE) on the full detector on a few microseconds window. A minimum of 6 Level 1 hits is typically required. In case of an event is found, all Level 1 and Level 0 hits of the full detector during the few microsecond correlation time window are written on disk, otherwise the data of these hits are thrown away. The main elements of the data acquisition and communication system of the ANTARES neutrino telescope are summarized in Fig.1.

Time Synchronization over Ethernet. One of the most critical aspects of deep-sea neutrino telescopes is the time synchronization. Sub-nanosecond synchronization between OMs is required in order to be able to reconstruct the muon track. ANTARES first [7] and KM3NeT later [8], have made a large effort to deal with this. Due to this need and effort, which is also of interest to other particle physics experiments, a new project, "White Rabbit" [9], is on the way in order to develop the equipment and protocols for having a sub-nanosecond timing synchronization over Ethernet. An international collaboration has been set with the participation of particle physics organizations, such as CERN, GSI, NIKHEF, and companies (Integrasys, Seven Solutions, GnuDD, Creotech, Elproma, National Instruments). To be specific, White Rabbit allows to time-tag measured data precisely and trigger data taking in large installations while at the same time use the same network to transmit data. It allows sub-nanosecond synchronization connecting thousands of nodes within typical distances of 10 km between nodes. It is fully open hardware, firmware and software allowing reliable gigabit rate Ethernet-based data transfer. It takes advantage of the latest developments on synchronous Ethernet and IEEE 1588 to enable the distribution of accurate timing information to the nodes saving noticeable amounts of bandwidth.

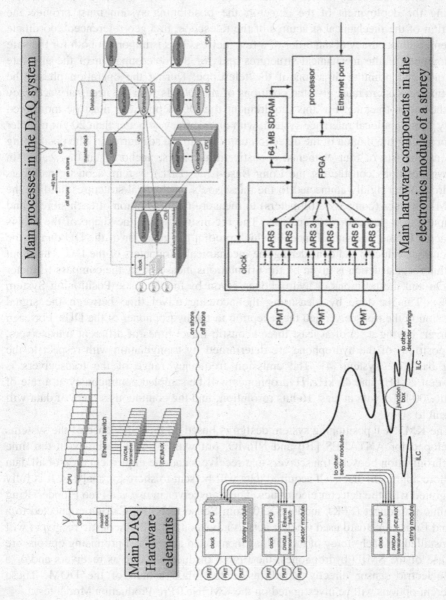

Fig. 1. Main elements of the data acquisition and communication system of the ANTARES neutrino telescope [5]

3.2   KM3NeT Acoustic Positioning and Monitoring System

A key element in a deep-sea neutrino telescope is the positioning system that must supply information for both the installation and operation phases of the detector. During the deployment of the detector, the positioning system must provide the position of the mechanical structures of the telescope, in a geo-referenced coordinate system, with accuracy of the order of a few metres. This is important both for the safe deployment of the mechanical structures and for the determination of the absolute position and pointing direction of the telescope. During the operation phase, the positioning system must give the positions of the DOMs with the necessary accuracy for the muon tracking. For this requirement the DOM positions must be monitored every 30 s, in a local reference system, with an accuracy of better than 20 cm in order to correct for the motion of the detection units due to the sea currents. The positioning system consists of four elements: acoustic transceivers, anchored on the seabed in known positions constituting the Long Base-Line (LBL) system; acoustic receivers (hydrophones) rigidly connected to the telescope's mechanical structures holding the DOMs; devices (compasses-tiltmeters) to measure the orientation of each storey; and computers on-shore for data analysis. The reconstruction of the shape of the DU is extracted by the mechanical models which predict the behavior of the DU due to the sea current velocity and considering the mechanical parameters of the DU. The input for this reconstruction is given by the orientations measured by the compass-tiltmeter system and the positions of hydrophones given by the Acoustic Positioning System (APS). This is done by measuring the acoustic travel time between the signal emission in the transceiver and the reception in the hydrophones of the DUs. For each receiver, having a set of at least three acoustic travel times of different transceivers, the positions of the hydrophone are determined by triangulation with respect to the long base-line system [4]. The emission frequency range of the transceivers is between 20 kHz and 45 kHz. Hydrophones will be sampled continuously at a rate of about 200 kHz, with at least 16 bits resolution, and the continuous stream of data will be sent to shore.

The KM3NeT positioning system design is based on the experience of the systems developed for ANTARES [10] and NEMO, but with a better accuracy in the time synchronization between transceivers and receivers and the implementation of all data to shore approach, that is all acquired data will be sent to shore for analysis. It is fully integrated with the detector electronics. The transceiver in use is a Free Flooded Ring ceramic transducer (FFR), model SX30 from Sensortech Ltd, Canada connected to a Sound Emission Board used when it acts as a beacon [11, 12]. Acoustic receivers will be installed on each storey of the DU, as mentioned above, and promising options are the use of the SMID hydrophones, the FFR transducers acting as receivers and/or a piezoelectric sensor directly glued inside the glass sphere of the DOM. These different options will be investigated on the KM3NeT Pre-Production Model test.

Both the acoustic receivers of the DUs and the LBL transceivers are synchronous and phased with respect to the master clock time signal transmitted from shore. This set-up allows also for the use of acoustic data for studies of acoustic neutrino detection and searches for acoustic and optical coincidences. It will also allow for monitoring of the environment around the detector and studies of Earth and Sea Science: biology, geophysics and oceanography. The scheme of the acoustic positioning and monitoring system is shown in Figure 2, together with the acoustic network and data management architecture of the acoustic monitoring system.

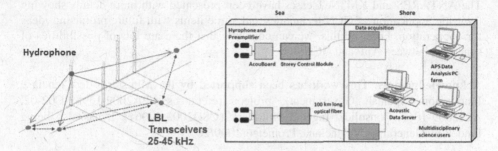

Fig. 2. Left: Scheme of the acoustic positioning system. The LBL is a geo-referenced system to identify the positions of acoustic receivers on the DU. The system is based on measurements of acoustic time of flight between transceivers and hydrophones. Right: Acoustic network and data management architecture of the acoustic monitoring system.

Sea Acoustic Monitoring Systems. Considering the number of acoustic sensors and the volume instrumented, the acoustic system planned for KM3NeT is certainly the most ambitious acoustic monitoring system at deep-sea. In this sense, it will constitute a unique observatory. However, it should not be understood as a separated item from other initiatives. Firstly, there is also a precedent of acoustic monitoring system in the ANTARES neutrino telescope, called AMADEUS [13]. It consists of 36 acoustic sensors distributed in 6 storeys of 2 ANTARES lines. This system was thought as a basic system to evaluate the feasibility of the acoustic neutrino detection technique, but it has also shown its capability for sea acoustic monitoring studies. Last, but not least, there is an initiative, LIDO-ESONET[8], which is a demonstrator for a broad network of acoustic monitoring systems at sea. AMADEUS is one of the nodes of this network. LIDO-ESONET has shown that it is possible to distribute the acoustic data from these monitoring systems through internet in almost real time. Recent advances in protocols and architecture systems, such as the ones discussed in [14, 15], may help to reach the final goal of linking all the nodes and sensors. Another critical aspect for the extension of these systems is the cost and complexity for cables and connectors of the sensors. There is a good opportunity for GCN technologies in this topic in order to develop more autonomous systems with higher efficiency, low power consumption and wireless communication [16]. In this sense, some efforts have been made in order to use standard wireless connections for short-distance water applications [17, 18]. With this approach, the cost and the number of failure points will be reduced significantly.

---

[8] http://www.esonet-noe.org/Main-activities/
Demonstration-missions/LIDO.

4   Summary and Conclusions

The scientific and technologic challenges of ApP have been presented, as well as their needs in GCN technologies. On the other hand, it has also been stressed that ApP facilities and experiments are good frames for developing and testing new GCN tools. The ANTARES and KM3NeT cases have been presented with more details showing the wide application of GCN techniques and some items with future promising ideas for cooperation. From all this, we can conclude that there are lots of possibilities of synergies between ApP and GCN.

Acknowledgments. This work has been supported by the Ministerio de Ciencia e Innovación (Spanish Government), project references FPA2009-13983-C02-02, ACI2009-1067, Consolider-Ingenio Multidark (CSD2009-00064). It has also being funded by Generalitat Valenciana, Prometeo/2009/26.

References

1. Ageron, M., et al.: (ANTARES Collaboration): ANTARES: The first undersea neutrino telescope. Nucl. Instrum. Meth. A 651, 11–38 (2011)
2. Ardid, M.: ANTARES: An Underwater Network of Sensors for Neutrino Astronomy and Deep-Sea Research. Ad Hoc & Sensor Wireless Networks 8, 21–34 (2009)
3. KM3NeT Consortium, Technical Design Report (2010), http://www.km3net.org ISBN: 978-90-6488-033-9
4. Bigongiari, C.: The KM3NeT Project for a Very Large Submarine Neutrino Telescope. Ad Hoc & Sensor Wireless Networks 8, 119–140 (2009)
5. Aguilar, J.A., et al.: (ANTARES Collaboration): The data acquisition system for the ANTARES neutrino telescope. Nucl. Instrum. Meth. A 570, 107–116 (2007)
6. Aguilar, J.A., et al.: (ANTARES Collaboration): Performance of the front-end electronics of the ANTARES neutrino telescope. Nucl. Instrum. Meth. A 622, 59–73 (2010)
7. Aguilar, J.A., et al.: (ANTARES Collaboration): Time calibration of the ANTARES neutrino telescope. Astroparticle Physics 34, 539–549 (2011)
8. Toscano, S., et al.: Time calibration and positioning for KM3NeT. Nucl. Instrum. Meth. A 602, 183–186 (2009)
9. Moreira, P., et al.: White Rabbit: Sub-Nanosecond Timing Distribution over Ethernet. In: ISPCS 2009 International IEEE Symposium on Precision Clock Synchronization for Measurement, Control and Communication, pp. 58–62. IEEE Press, New York (2009)
10. Ardid, M.: Positioning system of the ANTARES neutrino telescope. Nucl. Instrum. Meth. A 602, 174–176 (2009)
11. Ardid, M., et al.: Acoustic Transmitters for Underwater Neutrino Telescopes. Sensors 12, 4113–4132 (2012)
12. Llorens, C.D., et al.: The sound emission board of the KM3NeT acoustic positioning system. J. Instr. 7, C01001, 1–9 (2012)
13. Aguilar, J.A., et al.: (ANTARES Collaboration): AMADEUS—The acoustic neutrino detection test system of the ANTARES deep-sea neutrino telescope. Nucl. Instrum. Meth. A 626-627, 128–143 (2011)
14. Esposito, C., Cotroneo, D., Gokhale, A., Schmidt, D.: Architectural Evolution of Monitor and Control Systems - Issues and Challenges. Network Protocols and Algorithms 2(3), 1–17 (2010)

15. Sendra, S., Fernández, P.A., Quilez, M.A., Lloret, J.: Study and Performance of Interior Gateway IP routing Protocols. Network Protocols and Algorithms 2(4), 88–117 (2010)

16. Mohsin, A.H., Bakar, K.A., Adekiigbe, A., Ghafoor, K.Z.: A Survey of Energy-aware Routing protocols in Mobile Ad-hoc Networks: Trends and Challenges. Network Protocols and Algorithms 4(2), 82–107 (2012)

17. Lloret, J., Sendra, S., Ardid, M., Rodrigues, J.: Underwater Wireless Sensor Communications in the 2.4 GHz ISM Frequency Band. Sensors 12, 4237–4264 (2012)

18. Sendra, S., Lamparero, J.V., Lloret, J., Ardid, M.: Study of the Optimum Frequency at 2.4GHz ISM Band for Underwater Wireless Ad Hoc Communications. In: Li, X.-Y., Papavassiliou, S., Ruehrup, S. (eds.) ADHOC-NOW 2012. LNCS, vol. 7363, pp. 260–273. Springer, Heidelberg (2012)

Exploiting SCTP Multistreaming to Reduce Energy Consumption of Multiple TCP Flows over a WLAN

Masafumi Hashimoto, Go Hasegawa, and Masayuki Murata

Graduate School of Information Science and Technology, Osaka University, Japan
{m-hasimt,murata}@ist.osaka-u.ac.jp, hasegawa@cmc.osaka-u.ac.jp

Abstract. The energy efficiency of a wireless client is an important issue for wireless network environments. A common strategy for energy saving in wireless network devices is to remain in sleep mode when data are not being transmitted or received. However, when multiple TCP flows are established from a wireless client, determination and control of sleep timings are difficult. In addition, frequent state transitions between active and sleep modes consume energy, resulting in a reduction in energy efficiency. In this paper, we propose an energy-efficient method for multiple TCP flows in wireless LAN (WLAN) environments. The proposed method is termed SCTP tunneling, and aggregates multiple TCP flows into a single SCTP association between a wireless client and access point to control packet transmission and reception timings. Furthermore, SCTP tunneling lengthens sleep time by transmitting and receiving multiple packets in a bursty fashion. In this study, we construct a mathematical model of the energy consumed by SCTP tunneling to assess its energy efficiency. Through numerical examples, we show that the proposed method can reduce energy consumption by up to 69%.

Keywords: Transmission Control Protocol (TCP), Stream Control Transmission Protocol (SCTP), wireless LAN, energy efficiency.

1   Introduction

There is a great deal of interest in reducing the energy consumed through wireless communication. For energy saving in media access control (MAC) layer protocols, the IEEE 802.11 standard defines a power saving mode (PSM) [1], as opposed to the mode under normal operation, which is referred to as the continuously active mode (CAM). Although PSM can considerably reduce energy consumption, it can also degrade network performance characteristics such as throughput and latency [2].

Several researchers have proposed energy-efficient methods for wireless LANs (WLANs) [2–7]. Some of these methods [2–4] achieve high energy efficiency by mainly modifying MAC protocols, whereas the others [5–7] are energy-efficient solutions for specific applications. In contrast, we aim to derive a generalized transport-layer solution for energy saving without modifying the applications or MAC protocols.

In a typical environment where mobile devices are utilized, multiple TCP connections are established for concurrently running applications. In such a case, determination and control of sleep timings by the wireless client are difficult because packets of each TCP flow are transmitted and received independently. Moreover, this uncoordinated behavior produces frequent state transitions between the active and sleep modes

J. Lloret Mauri and J.J.P.C. Rodrigues (Eds.): GreeNets 2012, LNICST 113, pp. 102–111, 2013.

of a wireless network interface (WNI), which consumes extra energy, and results in the reduction of energy efficiency.

To overcome these issues, we propose an energy-efficient method for TCP data transfer over a WLAN in this paper. The key concept of the proposed method is that aggregate TCP packets are transmitted and received in a bursty fashion (known as *burst transmission*) to lengthen the idle time in which a WNI can enter sleep mode. To this end, the proposed method exploits stream control transport protocol (SCTP) [8] for TCP data transfer over a WLAN. We call this method *SCTP tunneling*. An SCTP association is established between a wireless client and an access point (AP), and all packets of TCP flows at the wireless client are aggregated into the association by means of SCTP multistreaming. Main contribution to save energy of SCTP tunneling is to reduce the number of state transitions between active and sleep modes, which is one factor of energy consumption, by burst transmission at transport-layer level. In practical cases, SCTP tunneling is used by combining it with sleep mechanisms at MAC-level such as PSM or automatic power save delivery (APSD) [1]. Note that energy wasted due to the behavior at MAC-level (e.g. frame collisions, overhearing, etc.) is out of scope of this work because it should be solved at MAC-level.

We derive an energy consumption model for SCTP tunneling to assess the potential gain in energy efficiency by its application. This model is based on our previous energy consumption model for a single TCP flow in a WLAN [9, 10], and focuses on both the frame exchanges of an IEEE 802.11 MAC and the detailed behavior of TCP congestion control mechanisms. [9] presented an energy consumption model for TCP data transfer over a WLAN, which was then extended to accommodate burst transmission in [10]. From the numerical results of the current model, we demonstrate the energy efficiency of SCTP tunneling for various aggregate throughputs of TCP flows.

2 SCTP Tunneling

The key concept of SCTP tunneling is that TCP packets of multiple flows at a wireless client are aggregated, and are transmitted or received in a bursty fashion to lengthen idle time in which the client can sleep during multiple TCP data transfer. Packet aggregation is realized by using SCTP, and thereby the transmission and reception timings are controlled with burst transmission.

2.1 TCP Flow Aggregation Using SCTP

SCTP is a connection-oriented transport protocol providing a service similar to TCP. In contrast to the stream-oriented nature of TCP, however, SCTP is message-oriented, and this feature is utilized in SCTP tunneling. Another feature of SCTP is multistreaming, which enables streams of user messages from multiple upper-layer applications to be multiplexed into a single SCTP association.

In SCTP tunneling, an SCTP association is established between a wireless client and an AP, as shown in Fig. 1. All packets of multiple TCP flows (e.g., the three flows in Fig. 1) are sent by SCTP tunneling, and each TCP flow is distinguished as a single stream in the SCTP association through multistreaming. Note that SCTP tunneling can

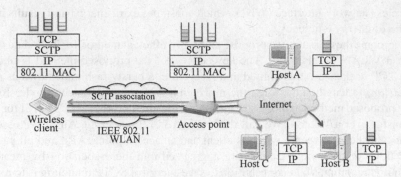

Fig. 1. SCTP tunneling in WLAN environment

also be applicable to UDP flows. A TCP packet generated in a wireless client is encapsulated in an SCTP-DATA chunk and enqueued in a transmission queue of the SCTP association. When a new SCTP packet can be transmitted, an SCTP-DATA chunk is dequeued from the transmission queue and is placed in a single SCTP packet. Transmission of the SCTP packet then obeys SCTP congestion control mechanisms. Once the SCTP packet is received by an AP, the packet is decapsulated and the original TCP packet is forwarded to its destination. At this time, SCTP at the AP generates an SCTP-SACK chunk to acknowledge receipt of the SCTP-DATA chunk. This SCTP-SACK chunk may piggyback with other SCTP-DATA chunks to the client. Data transmission from the AP to the client is conducted in a similar way to the above sequence.

By this method multiple TCP flows are aggregated, and thus the transmission and reception timings of multiple TCP packets can be controlled.

2.2   Burst Transmission

To lengthen the idle time in which a wireless client sleeps, SCTP tunneling employs burst transmission of SCTP packets by means of a delayed ACK mechanism applicable to SCTP. Figure 2 shows packet sequences of a wireless client during SCTP tunneling with and without burst transmission. If m SCTP packets are sent by burst transmission, these packets are transmitted and received consecutively by setting the delayed ACK parameter to m. In this case, once an SCTP has received m SCTP packets, in which the last packet contains an SCTP-SACK chunk, new m packets can be sent simultaneously. Upon receiving the SCTP packets including the SCTP-SACK chunk, another SCTP can consecutively send m new SCTP packets. By this mechanism, burst transmission can be realized. Note that an SCTP-SACK chunk piggybacks with an SCTP-DATA chunk in the mth SCTP packet. When the delayed ACK timer has expired, an SCTP packet containing an SCTP-SACK chunk is transmitted immediately. In the proposed method, we assume that the wireless client informs an AP of the value of m when establishing an SCTP association.

To send SCTP packets in bursts, SCTP tunneling buffers SCTP packets at the tunnel inlet until m TCP packets arrive, which results in an additional delay for each TCP

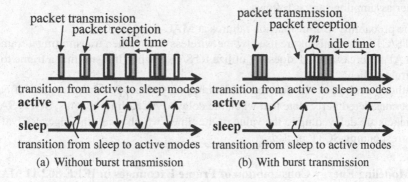

Fig. 2. Packet sequences of wireless client during SCTP tunneling

packet. Here, by using the average number of SCTP packets sent per unit time, R_{sctp}, the average buffering delay at the tunnel inlet is calculated as

$$D = \frac{m-1}{2} \frac{1}{R_{sctp}}. \tag{1}$$

SCTP tunneling thus enables a wireless client to save energy by sleeping during the idle time lengthened by burst transmission. In this paper, *ideal sleeping* is assumed when assessing the energy efficiency gained by SCTP tunneling. Ideal sleep implies that a WNI knows both the transmission and reception schedules of SCTP packets such that it can sleep and wake up with exact timing.

3   Energy Consumption Model

In this section, we construct an energy consumption model for SCTP tunneling. This model consists of two parts: a MAC-level submodel (Subsection 3.2) and an SCTP-level submodel (Subection 3.3). The assumptions for deriving these models are first described in Subection 3.1, after which the submodels are outlined.

3.1   Assumptions

The environment here is a WLAN in which a single SCTP association is established between a wireless client and an AP. Multiple TCP upstream and downstream flows are generated in the wireless client by applications. We assume that the average throughputs of TCP flows are given.

Suppose that at the hardware level the WNI has four communication modes — *transmit*, *receive*, *idle* or *listen*, and *sleep* [11]. Each of these modes has a different power consumption denoted by P^t, P^r, P^l, and P^s, respectively. Furthermore, the WNI consumes power when transiting between active and sleep modes, and we define P^{as} and P^{sa} as the power consumption when changing from and to active mode, respectively. The durations of these power consumptions are then denoted T^{as} and T^{sa}, respectively.

Other assumptions are as follows.

- The probability of transmission failures at MAC-level is given.
- RTS/CTS mechanisms are used by the wireless client when transmitting a frame to an AP, whereas and AP does not utilize RTS/CTS when transmitting a frame to the wireless client.
- Although values of the delayed ACK timer may affect performance, this effect is not considered here. Note that when the delayed ACK timer expires, SCTP-SACK packets are delayed up to the value of the timer, which result in longer RTT of the corresponding SCTP packets.

3.2   Modeling Energy Consumption of Frame Exchanges in IEEE 802.11 MAC

Due to space limitations, we omit the calculation process of expected times for a wireless client to send and receive one data frame, defined as $E[T^t]$ and $E[T^r]$, respectively, and the corresponding energy consumptions, denoted by $E[J^t]$ and $E[J^r]$, respectively. As a result, $E[T^t]$ and $E[T^r]$ are derived as follows:

$$E[T^t] = \sum_{i=1}^{N+1} \sum_{j=1}^{i} T^t(j)Q(i), \ E[T^r] = \sum_{i=1}^{N+1} \sum_{j=1}^{i} T^r(j)Q(i) \tag{2}$$

where N is a maximum number of data frame retransmissions, $T^t(i)$ and $T^r(i)$ are the average time by the wireless client to send and receive one data frame for the ith transmission, respectively, and $Q(i)$ is the probability that a data frame is transmitted i times. $T^t(i)$ and $T^r(i)$ are calculated as

$$T^t(i) = 3T_{SIFS} + T_{DIFS} + T^{BO}(i) + 4\tau + T_{RTS} + T_{DATA}^{client} + T_{CTS} + T_{ACK}, \tag{3}$$

$$T^r(i) = T_{SIFS} + T_{DIFS} + T^{BO}(i) + 2\tau + T_{DATA}^{AP} + T_{ACK} \tag{4}$$

where T_{SIFS} is the short interframe space (SIFS), T_{DIFS} is the distributed interframe space (DIFS), T_{RTS} is the transmission duration of the RTS frame, T_{CTS} is a transmission duration of the CTS frame, T_{DATA}^{client} and T_{DATA}^{AP} are transmission and reception duration of a data frame, respectively, T_{ACK} is reception duration of an ACK frame, $T^{BO}(i)$ is the average backoff time of the ith transmission after $(i-1)$ consecutive transmission failures, and τ is the radio propagation delay. $Q(i)$ is given by

$$Q(i) = \begin{cases} q^{i-1}(1-q) & \text{if } i \leq N \\ q^N & \text{if } i = N+1. \end{cases} \tag{5}$$

where q denotes the probability of transmission failure at MAC level.

Similarly, $E[J^t]$ and $E[J^r]$ are calculated as follows:

$$E[J^t] = \sum_{i=1}^{N+1} \sum_{j=1}^{i} J^t(j)Q(i), \ E[J^r] = \sum_{i=1}^{N+1} \sum_{j=1}^{i} J^r(j)Q(i) \tag{6}$$

where $J^t(i)$ and $J^r(i)$ are the energy consumptions for the ith data frame transmission and reception after $(i-1)$ failures, respectively. $J^t(i)$ and $J^r(i)$ are derived as

$$J^t(i) = P^l(3T_{SIFS} + T_{DIFS} + T^{BO}(i) + 4\tau) + P^t(T_{RTS} + T_{DATA}^{client}) + P^r(T_{CTS} + T_{ACK}), \tag{7}$$

$$J^r(i) = P^l(T_{SIFS} + T_{DIFS} + T^{BO}(i) + 2\tau) + P^t T_{ACK} + P^r T_{DATA}^{AP}. \tag{8}$$

3.3 Modeling Energy Consumption of SCTP Tunneling

The congestion control mechanisms for an SCTP association are the same as those in TCP. Therefore, we can regard the behavior of SCTP congestion control mechanisms as being that for a single TCP flow. As a result, the energy consumption model for SCTP tunneling is formulated based on that for a single TCP flow in [9, 10]. Specifically, we determine the energy consumption per unit time (i.e., the power consumption) for a WNI of the wireless client.

The behavior of congestion control mechanisms can be divided to two phases: the initial slow start phase and the congestion avoidance phase. As a simplification, the effects of slow start phase are not considered here because their contribution is considered sufficiently small [9, 10]. The congestion avoidance phase can further be divided into two periods: a triple duplicate (TD) period, which is the duration between two packet loss events detected by triple duplicate TCP-ACK packets; and a timeout (TO) period, which is the duration of a retransmission timeout (RTO) sequence. According to our previous studies [9, 10], the power consumption for a WNI of the wireless client is given by

$$P = \frac{J^{TD} + Q(E[W])J^{TO}}{E[A] + Q(E[W])E[Z^{TO}]} \tag{9}$$

where J^{TD} is the expected energy consumption of a TD period, J^{TO} is the expected energy consumption of a TO period, $Q(w)$ is the probability that a packet loss is detected by an RTO as a function of window size w, and $E[W]$ is the expected window size when the first packet loss occurs. J^{TD} and J^{TO} are as functions of Eqs. (2) and (6). Finally, $E[A]$ and $E[Z^{TO}]$ are the expected duration of TD and TO periods, respectively. Equations for J^{TD}, J^{TO}, $Q(w)$, $E[W]$, $E[A]$, and $E[Z^{TO}]$ were derived in [9, 10].

However, in [9, 10] $E[A]$ is calculated under the assumption that congestion control behavior is dependent on the average round trip time (RTT) of a TCP connection, whereas in SCTP tunneling this behavior is determined by the arrival rate of TCP packets. Due to space limitations, we omit the calculation process of $E[A]$. Using the the average number of SCTP packets sent per unit time through a single direction of SCTP tunneling, R_{sctp} (packet/s), $E[A]$ is calculated as

$$E[A] = \left(\frac{1-p}{p} + \frac{3}{2}E[W]\right)\frac{1}{R_{sctp}} \tag{10}$$

where p is the probability of packet drop events at the SCTP level, which is given by $p = q^{N+1}$. R_{sctp} is calculated as $R_{sctp} = \min\left(R, R_{sctp}^{max}\right)$ where R is the arrival rate of TCP packets (packet/s) and R_{sctp}^{max} is the maximum throughput (packet/s) achieved by the SCTP tunneling, which is given by $R_{sctp}^{max} = 1/(E[T^t] + E[T^r])$.

4   Numerical Results and Discussion

4.1   Parameter Settings

We consider an IEEE 802.11a WLAN in which multiple upstream and downstream TCP flows are established between a wireless client and wired hosts (Fig. 1). The WLAN

Table 1. WLAN parameters

Name	Value	Name	Value
Data rate	54 Mbps	PLCP preamble	16 μs
Slot time	9 μs	MAC header	24 B
SIFS	16 μs	LLC header	8 B
DIFS	34 μs	CW_{min}	15
		CW_{max}	1023

Table 2. Power consumption of Atheros AR5004 [12] and parameters of state transitions [2, 13]

P^t	P^r	P^l	P^s	P^{as}	P^{sa}	T^{as}	T^{sa}
1.4 W	0.9 W	0.8 W	0.016 W	0.8 W	1.4 W	1 μs	1 ms

parameters of IEEE 802.11a are summarized in Table 1. To calculate τ, we assume that the wireless client is located 4 m from the AP. From a data sheet for a WNI implemented by using the Atheros AR5004 chip [12] and measurement studies [2,13], we set parameters of power consumption to the values listed in Table 2. The TCP-DATA and TCP-ACK packet sizes are set to 1500 B and 40 B, respectively. The maximum number of frame retransmissions is set to $N = 7$.

4.2   Numerical Results

Figure 3 shows the power consumption results in the case that only upstream TCP flows exist when $q = 0.1$, 0.2, and 0.5. Here, we evaluate the performance of CAM and sleeping with burst transmission for $m = 1$, 2, and 5. Note that $m = 1$ signifies sleeping without burst transmission, while $m > 1$ is sleeping with burst transmission. In this figure, the x-axis represents the aggregate throughput of upstream TCP flows, where the average throughput of each TCP flow is 150 KB/s. The results when upstream and downstream TCP flows coexist show a similar trend to Fig. 3. Moreover, changes in q have little effect on the power consumption.

From Fig. 3, we observe that the power consumption when utilizing CAM is increased by an increase in the aggregate throughput of upstream TCP flows. As the aggregate throughput grows, the duration of packet transmission and reception increases and the idle time decreases. When sleeping is employed, the power consumption is considerably reduced regardless of the value of m. The power consumption is increased for large aggregate throughput, whereas the increase rate of power consumption is low at high m values. For instance, when the aggregate throughput of upstream TCP flows is about 500 KB/s in Fig 3, sleeping without burst transmission reduces power consumption by 27% compared with CAM. In contrast, the reduction is around 69% for sleeping with $m = 5$ because the smaller number of state transitions resulting from burst transmission has a large impact on energy reduction.

If aggregate throughput is further increased, the power consumption when using sleeping eventually surpasses the consumption for CAM, and approaches that without

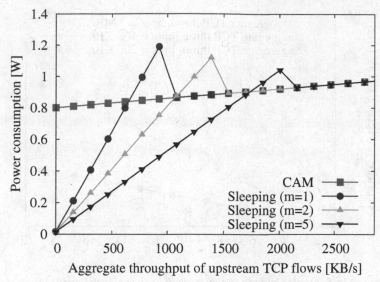

Fig. 3. Power consumption as a function of aggregate throughput of upstream TCP flows when $q = 0.1$ ($p = 1.00 \times 10^{-8}$)

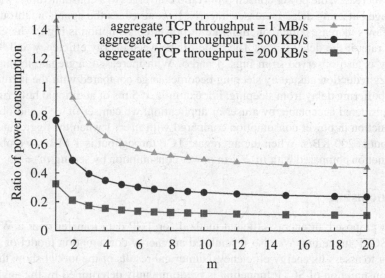

Fig. 4. Power consumption ratio for various m values and $q = 0.1$

sleeping. The power consumption required for state transitions exceeds the reduction realized by sleeping since the idle time is short. Note that such a situation can be avoided by staying in active mode when the idle time is insufficient.

Fig. 4 shows the power consumption ratio, obtained by dividing the power consumption when using sleeping by that when using CAM, for various m values and $q = 0.1$. Energy efficiency is high when the ratio is small. The corresponding average buffering delay which is calculated by Eq. (1) is presented in Fig. 5.

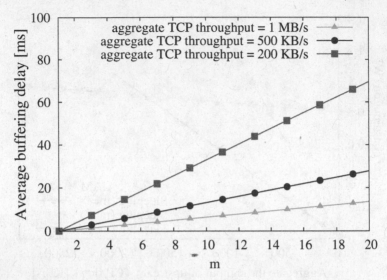

Fig. 5. Average buffering delay for various m values and $q = 0.1$

As m increases, the power consumption ratio converges to a constant value, whereas the average buffering delay increases linearly. In contrast, as the aggregate throughput of TCP flows increases, the reduction rate of power consumption is high, whereas the increase rate of the delay is low. The trade-off between energy efficiency and buffering delay is also observed from Figs. 4 and 5. With increased aggregate throughput, the energy reduction gained by sleeping becomes large compared with the increase of average buffering delay from sleeping. For example, if 5 ms of additional buffering delay is considered acceptable by a user or application, we can set $m = 2$ and obtain a 35% reduction in power consumption compared with $m = 1$ when the aggregate TCP throughput is 200 KB/s. When the aggregate TCP throughput is 1 MB/s, we obtain a 64% reduction compared with $m = 1$ in power consumption by setting $m = 8$.

5   Conclusion

We have proposed an energy-efficient method for TCP data transfer over a WLAN, termed SCTP tunneling. We also formulated an energy consumption model of SCTP tunneling to assess its energy efficiency. Numerical results of the model show that the power consumption of SCTP tunneling is predominantly determined by the aggregate throughput of TCP flows, while burst transmission can considerably reduce power consumption with increasing moderate delay.

In the future, we plan to implement the SCTP tunneling on commercial WLAN APs and wireless clients with power saving mode such as PSM and APSD.

Acknowledgment. This work was supported in part by the "Strategic Information and Communications R&D Promotion Programme (SCOPE)" of the Ministry of Internal Affairs and Communications (MIC), Japan, and by a Grant-in-Aid for JSPS Fellows, 24-2395, from the Japanese Society for the Promotion of Science.

References

1. IEEE 802.11-2007: Part 11: Wireless LAN Medium Access Control (MAC) and Physical Layer (PHY) specifications. IEEE (June 2007)
2. Krashinsky, R., Balakrishnan, H.: Minimizing energy for wireless web access with bounded slowdown. Wireless Networks 11, 135–148 (2005)
3. He, Y., Yuan, R.: A novel scheduled power saving mechanism for 802.11 wireless LANs. IEEE Transactions on Mobile Computing 8, 1368–1383 (2009)
4. Liu, J., Zhong, L.: Micro power management of active 802.11 interfaces. In: Proceedings of MobiSys 2008, pp. 146–159 (June 2008)
5. Yan, H., Watterson, S.A., Lowenthal, D.K., Li, K., Krishnan, R., Peterson, L.L.: Client-centered, energy-efficient wireless communication on IEEE 802.11b networks. IEEE Transactions on Mobile Computing 5, 1575–1590 (2006)
6. Namboodiri, V., Gao, L.: Energy-efficient VoIP over wireless LANs. IEEE Transactions on Mobile Computing 9, 566–581 (2010)
7. Dogar, F.R., Steenkiste, P., Papagiannaki, K.: Catnap: Exploiting high bandwidth wireless interfaces to save energy for mobile devices. In: Proceedings of MobiSys 2010, pp. 107–122 (June 2010)
8. Stewart, R.: Stream control transmission protocol. Request for Comments 4960 (September 2007)
9. Hashimoto, M., Hasegawa, G., Murata, M.: Modeling and analysis of power consumption in TCP data transmission over a wireless LAN environment. In: Proceedings of GreenComm 2011, pp. 1–6 (June 2011)
10. Hashimoto, M., Hasegawa, G., Murata, M.: Energy efficiency analysis of TCP with burst transmission over a wireless LAN. In: Proceedings of ISCIT 2011, pp. 292–297 (October 2011)
11. Atheros Communications, Power consumption and energy efficiency comparisons of wlan products. In Atheros White Papers (May 2003)
12. Wistron NeWeb Corp., CM9: WLAN 802.11 a/b/g mini-PCI Module, http://site.microcom.us/CM9.pdf
13. Andren, C., Bozych, T., Road, B., Schultz, D.: PRISM power management modes: Application note AN9665 (February 1997)

A Metropolitan-Scale Testbed
for Heterogeneous Wireless Sensor Networks
to Support CO$_2$ Reduction

Pablo E. Guerrero[1], Alejandro Buchmann[1], Kristof Van Laerhoven[1],
Immanuel Schweizer[1], Max Mühlhäuser[1], Thorsten Strufe[1],
Stefan Schneckenburger[2], Manfred Hegger[3], and Birgitt Kretzschmar[4]

[1] Dept. of Computer Science
[2] Botanical Garden, Dept. of Biology
[3] Energy Efficient Construction, Dept. of Architecture,
Technische Universität Darmstadt, Germany
[4] Environmental Agency, City of Darmstadt

Abstract. There exist two major contributions of network technology
to reduce CO$_2$ levels: reducing the energy consumption of the network
itself, and supporting areas of application to reduce CO$_2$ levels. The impact of the latter is potentially higher. Therefore, we present TUDμNet,
a testbed for a metropolitan-scale heterogeneous sensor network with
hundreds of nodes that help monitor and control CO$_2$ levels in urban
areas. Our testbed has four major application domains where it is being
applied: TU Darmstadt's award winning solar house, where temperature
and CO$_2$ levels are monitored; an 80 year old building in which a WSN
is deployed to measure ambient parameters that contribute to future
energy-saving remodeling; mobile sensors mounted on the streetcars of
the public tramway system to measure location-specific CO$_2$ levels that
are collected in a publicly accessible database to obtain CO$_2$ profiles; and
a hybrid sensor network in TUD's botanical garden to measure humidity, CO$_2$ levels and soil properties to improve the management of urban
parks. In this paper we present the concepts behind the design of our
testbed, its design challenges and our solutions, and potential applications of such metropolitan-scale sensor networks.

1 Introduction

The contributions of ICT to energy conservation, and given today's energy generation profile, to the lowering of greenhouse gas (GHG) emissions, and in particular CO$_2$ levels, has been widely debated and documented (e.g., in [8,5]). The
two main approaches are concisely characterized by the buzzwords *green ICT*
and *ICT for green*. The former refers to the reduction of power consumption of
ICT systems, while the latter refers to the use of ICT systems to reduce power
consumption in other application domains. Network technology, as one of the
basic building blocks of ICT systems, can be characterized in the same manner.

J. Lloret Mauri and J.J.P.C. Rodrigues (Eds.): GreeNets 2012, LNICST 113, pp. 112–120, 2013.
© Institute for Computer Sciences, Social Informatics and Telecommunications Engineering 2013

In this paper we address the problems of heterogeneous wireless sensor networks (WSNs) and their application in a variety of green application domains.

Research on sensor networks has largely concentrated on homogeneous setups under laboratory conditions, or single application deployments. Most deployments have been relatively small-scale and only recently large testbeds with few hundred nodes have been deployed (a comprehensive survey can be found in [2]). The testbed we discuss in this paper, TUDμNet [3], has several distinctive features. It is a metropolitan-scale hybrid sensor network that includes a variety of sensors on heterogeneous nodes, combines wireless and wired as well as stationary and mobile sensor nodes, permits running different applications on the same testbed, can be segmented through the use of scopes, and allows easy software deployment without manual restarting of the widely distributed sensor nodes. TUDμNet is being deployed in four domains, each addressing different *green* concerns and at the same time presenting their own realistic challenges.

The four green application domains addressed here are:

- The instrumentation of new, energy conscious buildings, realized in the testbed by instrumenting the award-winning solar house developed by the architecture department of the Technische Universität Darmstadt (TUD). Sensor nodes placed inside the house and attached at the house's façade measure environmental conditions to characterize how the house responds to these.
- The instrumentation of old buildings in which no infrastructure for sensor deployment exists and where WSNs are a cheap and effective way to collect data that can be used for energy-conservation measures and future energy-conscious renovation. This has been realized by deploying a sensor network in the large, 80 year old building of the CS Dept.
- The deployment of mobile, wireless sensor nodes on the streetcars of Darmstadt's public tramway transportation system to collect location-specific temperature data and CO$_2$ levels to build micro climate maps and the use of existing sensor infrastructure in Darmstadt for traffic management.
- The deployment of sensor nodes in open spaces that monitor humidity, solar radiation, temperature, soil properties, and CO$_2$ levels in TUD's botanical garden. Observations gained in this kind of deployment can enable an early and targeted response to environmental stress or dangers caused by the lack of water or fertilizers, and more generally to optimize the management of parks, the green lungs of urban areas.

Finally, the integration of the various domains allows us to study another set of interesting problems derived from the interplay of heterogeneous stationary/mobile and wireless/wired sensor nodes, and the integration and management of streams of sensor data.

The remainder of this paper addresses the challenges that are encountered in setting up a testbed in the four environments described above (Section 2). It then presents some details on how we addressed those challenges, and shows solutions that are implemented in TUDμNet to permit multiple applications and flexible and efficient software deployment in a metropolitan area sensor network, along with details of actual deployments and a sample of the data that can be obtained and the information that can be derived (Section 3). We conclude in Section 4 with an outlook.

2   Challenges

2.1   Testbed Services

Sensor network testbeds have been proposed as an intermediate solution between simulators and final deployments because these enable a rapid experimental evaluation of networked applications without having to physically re-deploy sensor nodes with every iteration. Essentially, testbeds offer two services: a) quick and robust software reprogramming of the underlying sensor platform under test, and b) reliable experiment data logging for its posterior evaluation. The heterogeneity of the underlying sensor platforms in terms of processing capabilities, physical and virtual communication possibilities, mobility patterns, as well as the physical positions of the nodes in the environment to ensure sensing coverage [9], among others, makes the realization of these two simple services a non-trivial endeavor. Moreover, exploratory experimentation, typical of embedded systems' software evaluation, means that the results of an initial version of an experiment's application can lead to a series of adjustments, which in turn must be executed on-demand on the testbed. This places additional non-functional requirements on the quality of service of the testbed, namely the need to assist testbed users with the experiment definition (e.g., site selection, node type selection, job scheduling, experiment parameter validation), provide adequate access control mechanisms to each deployment/site, support for concurrent experiment execution, and tools for an automated evaluation and visualization of the parameters of interest.

Testbeds resort to an extra hardware and/or software support layer between the underlying sensor platform and the testbed coordination server to fulfill their tasks. Although in certain setups the design of this support layer is constrained (e.g. in heritage buildings, network cabling through a façade might be not allowed, thus a wireless backend will be preferred, while a hospital deployment might forbid yet another wireless system), identifying its correct footprint has a big impact on the initial investment as well as the maintenance costs of the organizations running the testbed.

2.2   Application-Domain Level

Metropolitan areas typically span a number of different environments which offer varying potential for eliminating or reducing energy inefficiencies: urban areas with legacy buildings, green parks, commercial/industrial districts, and even new neighborhoods following modern construction techniques. A testbed must therefore match these areas with corresponding experimentation playgrounds that remain of a manageable scale, yet offer enough scientific fidelity to yield results applicable to other, similar environments. We next describe the challenges of a number of application domains which we are currently pursuing for the improvement of the energy efficiency.

Energy Efficient House Construction. The emergence of decentralized, micro-scale renewable energy sources (especially photovoltaic and geothermal heating/cooling) has led the sustainable construction of energy efficient residential homes into an interdisciplinary area of investigation beyond architecture and civil engineering, prompting ICT systems to come into play. The explosion of construction techniques and modern materials mobilized researchers and practitioners to establish a biennial competition, the Solar Decathlon [10], where participants measure their innovations applied to residential properties at a number of contests. These houses represent the state-of-the-art in low ecological footprint.

While many construction aspects are designed and validated through models and simulation, critical aspects of the construction remain unclear until a prototype is built: do the HVAC systems work as expected throughout the inner space of the house? are the (costly) materials of the ceiling and exterior walls correctly designed to tolerate the weather conditions to which they are effectively exposed (varying temperature and humidity levels)? are solar panels acting optimally and delivering the maximum amount of energy as originally planned? does the geothermal heat pump tunneling deliver the expected water temperature? These questions represent only some of the engineering challenges where WSNs offer an unprecedented monitoring resolution and can help to improve their energy consumption.

Old Buildings. In Europe, around 40% of energy consumption is due to building usage [7]. Buildings also are the largest source of CO_2 emissions [4]. Since energy usage is mostly caused during the operational stage (i.e. during user occupation), sensor networks become a key element for monitoring building usage and enabling intelligent (e.g. HVAC) control.

Public Transportation Systems. Transportation is responsible for approximately one third of the carbon dioxide emissions in the US. While policy makers are looking for more energy-efficient cars and alternative energy sources, a large amount of savings can come from smarter traffic management reducing traffic congestions [1]. As population density increases, it becomes a necessity to cope with increasing traffic.

To enable real-time traffic management for smart cities, data from different sources must be considered; counting cars is a first step, but not enough. To regulate traffic in real-time, knowledge about the amount and speed of cars is needed, together with projected traffic densities, wind speed and direction, microclimate in a given region, emission levels and a mechanism to reroute traffic. All of this data can only be collected on a metropolitan scale and might not be available from one provider.

Urban Park Management. Parks, squares and other open spaces are ever more important in metropolitan areas due to their effect in reducing environmental pollution, besides encouraging citizens to an active lifestyle and reducing stress through the interaction with nature. Urban park monitoring operations (open spaces, water streams, visitor counts), park irrigation and other maintenance tasks like lawn-mowing, pruning of trees, bushes and plants, and emptying garbage bins, all offer room for optimization.

2.3 Data Management

Cities often have a sensor infrastructure in place, and are becoming smarter by equipping themselves with a rising number of data sources from sensor nodes and mobile applications. Today, this data is application- and consumer-specific, and most importantly, closed (to government partners). The potential economic and societal value of these large data sets is slowly being uncovered through novel applications from businesses and other organizations (e.g. [11]) that reveal new exploitation schemes. This requires a new infrastructure that can cope with the volume of these data sources and is based on open data, standards and APIs.

3 Solutions

In this section we describe the general approach to experimentation through the federated testbed and two representative testbed deployments.

3.1 Architecture for Testbed Services

Figure 1 presents the high level architecture used in TUDμNet. Users define and schedule test jobs through a server, which offers a web interface and a set of scripts. The server interacts with a set of gateways, which control and assist the low-power sensor node layer. Each site is interconnected to the testbed server via MANDa, the metropolitan area network of the city of Darmstadt. Domain differences between sites of a federated testbed require alternative networking solutions for the support layer. While one site exploits the available Ethernet infrastructure, others need to resort to a wireless off-band channel for performing management tasks (cf. site 1 and 2, respectively, in Fig. 1). This infrastructure can also provide power to the sensor nodes, e.g., through USB cabling. Yet, in other sites, this ideal, dual layer instrumentation might be impossible/unfeasible (site 3), having to resort to in-band testbed service protocols, like Deluge, for reprogramming, and CTP for collecting data, and even to solar power, ensuring mobile nodes have energy for certain periods of time.

Experimentation through a testbed requires fine grain control of the test jobs. This includes definition of job execution times, selection of sensor and node types, network topology and geographical node distribution, among others. TUDμNet adopts the concept of *scopes* [6] to specify groups of nodes. Each user might have access to a different set of sites, or scopes, which together with a time quota enables spatio-temporal sharing of the overall system.

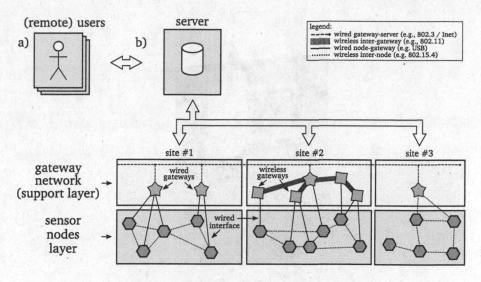

Fig. 1. High-level Testbed Architecture

3.2 Deployment on Streetcars

In order to generate a micro climate map for Darmstadt, we deployed a testbed of six wireless sensor nodes on the trams. By using mobile vehicles we can capture a large area using only a small amount of nodes. The six wireless nodes, manufactured by Libelium in Spain, are equipped with an 868 MHz transceiver for a metropolitan scale wireless range of over one kilometer.

The nodes are equipped with a temperature sensor, GPS for accurate localization, and most importantly solar cells (cf. Fig. 2). By using energy-efficient algorithms and an adaptive sampling rate [12], we are able to allow almost perpetual network operation even though the nodes are battery powered. A base station located in the city center collects all measurements as the trams pass by. They are then transmitted to the da_sense platform via GPRS.

3.3 Piloty Building Deployment

This testbed deployment is located in the building of the CS Dept. of the TUD, a 3-story building consisting mainly of office rooms. The site currently spans 30 offices at the north wing, each with 2 to 4 sensor nodes: TelosB and Zolertia Z1, equipped with an MSP430 MCU, an 802.15.4 radio operating at 2.4GHz, 48 to 92 kB of ROM, and 8 to 10 kB of RAM (respectively). The sensors attached to the nodes can measure temperature, humidity, light intensity, acceleration and CO$_2$. Figure 3 depicts a typical deployed office. In each, a Buffalo WZR-HP-G300N acts as gateway (green), which bridges departmental ethernet with the nodes (red) through a USB backchannel (red lines). This rather unconstrained environment has shown its own challenge: the USB backchannel.

Fig. 2. Sensor node deployed on a streetcar in Darmstadt

Fig. 3. An office at the CS building, with installed wireless sensors (red circles) that are also attached to a gateway (green) for quick reprogramming

3.4   Data Integration and Management

In order to organize the information produced in our deployments, we have developed a lightweight data layer, da_sense [1], that connects different sensor sources and allows visualization and correlation of all the data sources available through a standardized API. da_sense integrates most of the data streams described in

---

[1] http://www.da-sense.de

Fig. 4. Traffic data from inductive loops in Darmstadt's intersections

this paper and offers an open API to further innovate on the data. It also correlates different data streams (e.g. sound pressure and traffic density) to create virtual sensor nodes. Additional data sources can also be plugged into it. An example directly related to the traffic management application are Darsmtadt's street intersections, which are equipped with a large number of inductive loops that monitor the number of cars passing by and the utilization of the sensor in a 15-minute interval. We receive this data at da_sense, make it available for public consumption, visualize it (cf. Fig. 4) and correlate it with other data sources, leading to overall better optimizations.

4   Outlook

In this paper we have presented our ongoing work in designing, deploying and federating sensor network testbeds in domains that present great potential for reducing energy consumption and CO$_2$ levels. The data sets produced so far are gaining attention, and the testbed has already seen its first users external to the TUD. The streetcar deployment is being replicated in Hanoi, Vietnam, to enable online monitoring of traffic-generated pollution data, which further evidences the usefulness of the overall system. In the future, we plan to develop a number of applications to further exploit each site's sensors and which will run as permanent test jobs at TUDμNet.

Acknowledgments. We gratefully acknowledge funding support for this research. It was sponsored in part by the Priority Program on *Cooperative Sensor Communication* (Cocoon) in the context of the LOEWE Excellence Initiative of the State of Hesse, and in part by the PhD Training Group GRK 1362 *Cooperative, Adaptive and Responsive Monitoring in Mixed Mode Environments*

(GKmM) of the Deutsche Forschungsgemeinschaft. We also acknowledge the help of Iliya Gurov and Guillermo Gómez Almeida during the installation of the sensors.

References

1. Barth, M., Boriboonsomsin, K.: Real-World Carbon Dioxide Impacts of Traffic Congestion. Journal of the Transportation Research Board 2058(1), 163–171 (2010)
2. Gluhak, A., Krco, S., Nati, M., Pfisterer, D., Mitton, N., Razafindralambo, T.: A Survey on Facilities for Experimental Internet of Things Research. IEEE Communications Magazine 49(11), 58–67 (2011)
3. Guerrero, P.E., Buchmann, A., Khelil, A., Van Laerhoven, K.: TUDμNet, a Metropolitan-Scale Federation of Wireless Sensor Network Testbeds. In: 9th European Conference on Wireless Sensor Networks, EWSN 2012 (February 2012)
4. Hannus, M., Kazi, A.S., Zarli, A. (eds.): ICT Supported Energy Efficiency in Construction. REEB Project Consortium (February 2010)
5. Hilty, L., Coroama, V.: Energy Consumed vs. Energy Saved by ICT: A Closer Look. In: 23rd. Intl. Conference on Informatics for Environmental Protection, pp. 353–361. Shaker Verlag, Aachen (2009)
6. Jacobi, D., Guerrero, P.E., Petrov, I., Buchmann, A.: Structuring Sensor Networks with Scopes. In: 3rd IEEE European Conference on Smart Sensing and Context, EuroSSC 2008, Zurich, Switzerland (October 2008)
7. Maloney, C.: Foreword. In: 2nd. EEB Data Models Community Workshop, Sophia Antipolis, France, p. 6 (October 2011)
8. Mattern, F., Staake, T., Weiss, M.: ICT for Green: How Computers Can Help Us to Conserve Energy. In: 1st Int. Conference on Energy-Efficient Computing and Networking, pp. 1–10. ACM, New York (2010)
9. Mulligan, R.: Coverage in Wireless Sensor Networks: A Survey. Network Protocols and Algorithms 2(2), 27–53 (2010)
10. US Dept. of Energy. Solar Decathlon (2009), http://www.solardecathlon.org
11. Open Data Institute. The ODI Business Plan (May 2012), http://theodi.org
12. Schweizer, I., Fleischhacker, N., Muhlhäuser, M., Strufe, T.: SDF - Solar-aware Distributed Flow in Wireless Sensor Networks. In: 36th IEEE Conference on Local Computer Networks, pp. 382–390 (October 2011)

Author Index